Governing Affective
Citizenship

FRONTIERS OF THE POLITICAL

Series Editor:

Engin Isin is Professor of International Politics, Queen Mary University of London (QMUL) and University of London Institute in Paris (ULIP). He is a leading scholar of citizenship studies and is a Chief Editor of the journal Citizenship Studies. He is author and editor of eleven books in the field, including 'Being Political' and 'Citizens Without Frontiers'.

This series aims to contribute to our understanding of transversal political struggles beyond and across the borders of the nation-state, and its institutions and mechanisms, which have become influential and effective means of both contentious politics and political subjectivity. The series features titles that eschew and even disavow interpreting these transversal political struggles with categories and concepts.

Postcolonial Transitions in Europe: Contexts, Practices and Politics
Edited by Sandra Ponzanesi and Gianmaria Colpani
Citizenship and Place: Case Studies on the Borders of Citizenship
Edited by Cherstin M. Lyon and Allison F Goebel
The Question of Political Community: Sameness, Logos, Space
Jonna Pettersson
Postcolonial Intellectuals in Europe: Academics, Artists, Activists and their Publics,
  edited by Sandra Ponzanesi and Adriano José Habed
Citizen Journalism as Conceptual Practice: Postcolonial Archives and Embodied Political Acts of New Media
Bolette B. Blaagaard
Governing Affective Citizenship: Denaturalization, Belonging, and Repression
Marie Beauchamps

Governing Affective Citizenship

Denaturalization, Belonging, and Repression

Marie Beauchamps

ROWMAN & LITTLEFIELD
INTERNATIONAL

New York • London

Published by Rowman & Littlefield International Ltd
6 Tinworth Street, London SE11 5AL, United Kingdom
www.rowmaninternational.com

Rowman & Littlefield International Ltd.is an affiliate of Rowman & Littlefield
4501 Forbes Boulevard, Suite 200, Lanham, Maryland 20706, USA
With additional offices in Boulder, New York, Toronto (Canada), and Plymouth (UK)
www.rowman.com

British Library Cataloguing in Publication Data
A catalogue record for this book is available from the British Library

ISBN: HB 978-1-7866-0677-8

Library of Congress Cataloging-in-Publication Data

Names: Beauchamps, Marie, 1984- author.
Title: Governing affective citizenship : denaturalization, belonging, and
 repression / Marie Beauchamps.
Description: Lanham, Maryland : Rowman & Littlefield International, [2018] |
  Series: Frontiers of the political | Includes bibliographical references
  and index.
Identifiers: LCCN 2018040428 (print) | LCCN 2018050732 (ebook) | ISBN
  9781786606785 (electronic) | ISBN 9781786606778 (cloth : alk. paper)
Subjects: LCSH: Citizenship—Social aspects—France. | Citizenship, Loss
  of—France. | National security—Social aspects—France. |
  Rhetoric—Political aspects—France. | National characteristics,
  French—Political aspects.
Classification: LCC JN2919 (ebook) | LCC JN2919 .B43 2018 (print) | DDC
  323.60944—dc23
LC record available at https://lccn.loc.gov/2018040428

♾™ The paper used in this publication meets the minimum requirements of American
National Standard for Information Sciences—Permanence of Paper for Printed Library
Materials, ANSI/NISO Z39.48-1992.

Printed in the United States of America

Contents

Acknowledgments

This book began as my doctoral dissertation, which I defended in 2015, at the Amsterdam School for Cultural Analysis (ASCA), University of Amsterdam. Coincidentally, the year 2015 marked the hundredth anniversary of denaturalization law in France, turning the defense of my dissertation into an occasion to celebrate this historic moment within the sound of critique. I thank ASCA for giving me the gift of time and space to do uninterrupted research, during which I enjoyed Mireille Rosello's priceless supervision. I thank her most heartedly. Sincere thanks to my committee members: Louise Amoore, Robin Celikates, Marieke de Goede, Engin Isin, Christoph Lindner, and Sandra Ponzanesi.

Besides ASCA's vibrant research community, the project benefited from a close collaboration with a number of research networks, for which I am most grateful: the European Security Culture Project conducted by Marieke de Goede at the University of Amsterdam; the Literature and Law research group conducted by Frans-Willem Korsten and Yasco Horsman at Leiden University; the *Oecumene Project* conducted by Engin Isin at the Open University (UK); the Centre for Political Theory at the Université Libre de Bruxelles, directed by Justine Lacroix; the 2013 European International Relations Summer School *Security, Borders and Mobility* jointly organized in Brussels (BE) by the University of Kent's Brussels School of International Relations, King's College London and Sciences Po Paris and led by Didier Bigo and Tugba Basaran; and the University of London Institute in Paris, then directed by Andrew Hussey. Furthermore, I conducted archival research in the French National Archives (Paris), in the French National Library (BNF, Paris), and in the Library of the French National Assembly (Paris). Special thanks to Eloe Kingma, Jantine van Gogh, Patricia Pisters, Tim Yaczo, Niall Martin, Hanneke Stuit, Mikki Stelder, Thijs van den Berg, Noa Roei,

Sruti Bala, Johan Hartle, Astrid van Weyenberg, Pepita Hesselberth, Marijn Hoijtink, Gavin Sullivan, Stephanie Simon, Tessa de Zeeuw, Deena Dajani, Jef Huysmans, Teresa Pullano, Emmanuel-Pierre Guittet, Philippe Bonditti, Matthias Leese, Sharon Weinblum, Stef Wittendorp, Sarah Perret, Bruno Magalhães, Isabel Hollis, Sandra Mantu, Patricia de Vries, Bram Creusen, and Lucy Hall for your wonderful collegiality, openness, encouragements, and critical thoughts during all phases of this project. Your voices resonate as multiple echoes in my memory of its development, from its conception to its completion. So do the voices of all who made conferences and summer schools such inspiring and invigorating moments.

I most sincerely thank Dhara Snowden, my editor at Rowman & Littlefield International, and Engin Isin, my series editor, for making this happen. Many thanks to Rebecca Anastasi for her assistance throughout, and to Chloe Batch for the wonderful cover design.

Deepest thanks to Esther Peeren, Alexandra Gerny, Malu Peeters, and Lukas Hoex for reading parts of the manuscript when I was doing the final revisions, and to Engin Isin for reading the manuscript as a whole in its most final stage.

Last but not least, my gratitude goes to my friends and family, for having my back. Lukas, and Pablo, thank you for being there with me.

For reasons of legibility, I have provided only the English translations of French quotations from primary material and scholarly sources. Unless otherwise indicated, all translations are mine. In order to retain the poetic voice of epigraphs, however, I've chosen to keep those citations untranslated.

Some of the material to follow has found its way to publication in other venues, although in most instances significant alterations have been made. Thanks to the anonymous reviewers for their critical reading and sharp arguments. I acknowledge the following permissions to reprint:

Portions of the introduction appeared in my article "The Forfeiture of Nationality in France: Discursive Ambiguity, Borders, and Identities," *Space and Culture*, 19 (1) (2016) http://journals.sagepub.com/doi/full/10.1177/1206331214560091.

Chapter 3 has been published in a somewhat different version as "Olympe de Gouges's Trial and the Affective Politics of Denaturalization in France," *Citizenship Studies*, 20 (8) (2016) www.tandfonline.com/doi/full/10.1080/13621025.2016.1229195. Thanks to Jessica Merolli and Michael Di Gregorio for putting together such a fascinating issue on affective citizenship.

Chapter 5 figures as part of my article in *Space and Culture* cited above.

Portions of chapter 6 and chapter 7 have appeared as "Modelling the Self, Creating the Other: French Denaturalisation Law on the Brink of World War II" in the edited volume *Security/Mobility: Politics of Movement*, edited by

Matthias Leese and Stef Wittendorp, Manchester: Manchester University Press (2017).

Most of chapter 8 has been published as "Perverse Tactics: 'Terrorism' and National Identity in France," *Culture, Theory and Critique*, 58 (1) (2017) http://www.tandfonline.com/doi/full/10.1080/14735784.2015.1137480.

Introduction

Unless there is vigilance about [citizenship] rights ... corporate and state authorities will violate them in the name of commercial or security interests.

—Engin Isin and Peter Nyers (2014, 10)

Dénaturaliser, c'est mettre à l'épreuve ce lien entre l'individu et l'État en rappelant l'incertitude des conditions de national et d'étranger.

—Claire Zalc (2016)

The temporary or permanent withdrawal of citizenship has emerged as a measure of security in a number of states in Europe, as well as in the United States, Canada, and Australia. For instance, in the UK, no less than 150 British citizens have been deprived of their citizenship in response to the London and Manchester attacks of 2017. In 2017, in the Netherlands, the first chamber of Parliament approved a bill allowing the state, in the interest of national security, to revoke the Dutch citizenship of citizens participating in a terrorist organization. In France, then-president François Hollande announced his determination to expand the state's power to denaturalize citizens in his official address on November 16, 2015, three days after the terrorist attacks on civilian public places in Paris. Although current president Emmanuel Macron had initially criticized Hollande's initiative, there is no sign that he will revoke the already existing possibilities for the state to deprive citizens of their French nationality. To the contrary, his new counterterrorism policies show an increasing tendency to insert exceptional security measures into common law.

Depending on the context, temporary or permanent withdrawals of citizenship are known by legal terms such as "denationalization," "withdrawal," "deprivation," "revocation," "forfeiture," or "annulment of nationality and/or citizenship" (Gibney 2017; Mantu 2015; Macklin 2014; Weil 2013). This book gathers all these terms under the label "denaturalization" since it is immediately recognizable. However, the book's scope is to especially focus on the French sanction of *déchéance*, of which important parts of the meaning and connotations get lost in translation. This term *déchéance* expresses a demotion, a moral downgrading, and connotes biblical images representing those *déchus*, unworthy of paradise, dismissed and abjured to work their way on earth by means of hard labor and pain, as opposed to having an endless pleasurable life in paradise. *Déchéance* also expresses the deprivation of rights, be it the deprivation of civil rights or the rights attached to the exercise of a public function, such as to a member of parliament. In practice, the *déchéance* of nationality is a penal sanction leading to someone's loss of national citizenship. It differs, however, from a mere loss of nationality or citizenship, which is, strictly speaking, a civil consequence. Even though the effects are the same—someone's loss of national citizenship—the registers differ. While uncovering the genealogies of *déchéance*, this book draws on a broader repertoire in order to reveal the operational logics of denaturalization as a technology of government.

The focus on France and its debates on denaturalization has a theoretical purpose: France was one of the first countries to promulgate citizenship as a universal concept and to establish an assimilationist model of nationhood. Whether ardently cherished or vehemently contested, France's model occupies a seminal place in the history of nationality and citizenship. Scrutinizing the history of denaturalization in France thus contributes to understanding the foundations of ideas of citizenship and nationality. Furthermore, from a methodological point of view, the focus on one particular country allows in-depth insights into the genealogies of denaturalization and their impact on current political processes.

At the same time, the analysis's relevancy stretches beyond France. In light of contemporary developments, it has become clear that, as a technology of government, denaturalization is not (or no longer) specifically French but has become nested in politics of nationality and citizenship worldwide. In showing how the definition of terror, the terrorist, and terrorism overlap with the category of the stranger, the analysis offers a critical tool to read contemporary discourses where questions of citizenship rights are presented in relation to immigration and security. Even though the details of how denaturalization is used might differ from one context to another, this book offers a critical method to understand the general logic of denaturalization; it shows that denaturalization is a system of thought that influences seminal cultural political values, such as community, nationality, citizenship, selfhood, and otherness.

Embarking on a research journey involves heading toward an unknown destination. In this case, the unknown, which made itself known through archival research and practices of reading and interpretation, emerged as the role of affect and emotions. Studying denaturalization led me to discover, time and time again, how language and emotions contribute to the performativity of norms; it made me see that politics of nationality and citizenship are profoundly affective, and that affective citizenship belongs to deep-seated modes of the governing mechanisms of belonging and repression. When governmental language identifies an "other" as threatening, technologies of enclosure no longer foster feelings of togetherness or inclusion but instead institute affective mechanisms of rejection and repression. Thus, while denaturalization prominently appears as an instrumental frame to maintain and secure the national community, its effect is not security as such. Instead, denaturalization turns nationality and citizenship into affective technologies of government, turning questions of inclusion and exclusion into matters of belonging and repression. Accordingly, the book's focus on the affective dimension of denaturalization is an invitation to use the concept of affective citizenship as an analytical tool to look differently at military responses to terrorist attacks and political responses to immigration crises.

CONTEMPORARY POLITICAL EVENT: AN INTRODUCTION TO DENATURALIZATION

I first came to reflect on the meaning of denaturalization based on the following political event. In Grenoble, on July 30, 2010, then-President Nicolas Sarkozy addressed an assembly of top civil servants and police representatives. Flanked by the minister of home affairs, Brice Hortefeux, and the minister of justice, Michèle Alliot-Marie, Sarkozy made his speech after a series of violent riots and skirmishes between police and the inhabitants of Grenoble. According to media reports, the riots took place on the outskirts of Grenoble, in a notorious area called the Quartier de la Villeneuve, with a high concentration of poor-quality social housing. The violence increased after the police shot Karim Boudouda dead while he was fleeing with a cashbox stolen from a casino. In the midst of the clashes that continued during the following days and nights, the police reported having been targeted by firearms.

Titled "Discourse on the Theme of Fighting Insecurity," Sarkozy's response to the violence in Grenoble started by announcing the ministerial determination to set up a security-driven network of control intended to annihilate each and every criminal resident on French territory. First and foremost, the speech revealed an extreme political will to govern the people of France, in general, by means of instituting technologies of control such as cameras and electronic bracelets. Gradually, however, the main criminal targeted was explicitly defined as a person of foreign origin. Betraying a discursive conflation of immigration and security policies within French politics, the president announced: "It must be acknowledged that we are suffering from fifty years of insufficiently regulated immigration, which resulted in a failure of the integration system" (Sarkozy 2010, 22:58).

Deliberately linked to immigration, the reference to criminality establishes a specific normative cluster of identity according to which "the foreigner becomes compressed into state-determined categories ... by reference of insecurity" (Guild 2009, 2). Combining immigration and insecurity into one single area of political concern, Sarkozy's utterance reflects the much discussed conflation of immigration law and criminal law. Not only do European security policies increasingly include measures against illegal immigration practices, but migrants themselves tend to be framed as a generalized threatening other disturbing a European ideal of conduct that in itself remains utterly fictive (Guild 2009; Huysmans 2006; Jansen, Celikates, and de Bloois 2015; Valluy 2008).[1]

Labeling such conflation the "securitization of immigration" and thereby denoting the fact that states have taken control of immigration issues by designating it a security problem (Wæver 1995, 54), Jef Huysmans notes that "'migration' and related labels such as 'foreigner' and 'asylum seeker' [have become] politically powerful signifiers in contemporary Europe" (2000, 761). He thereby understands that the terms "foreigner" and "asylum seeker" "have a capacity to connect the internal security logic to the big political questions of cultural and racial identity" (761). Furthermore, "[social] and political agencies use the theme of immigration, foreigners, asylum-seekers and refugees to interrelate a range of disparate political issues in their struggle over power, resources and knowledge" (761). On the one hand, the restrictive and isolating contexts of security policies frame migrants negatively; on the other, the reduction of their identity to state-determined categories is being used as the connecting logic of contemporary politics.

Against this backdrop, Sarkozy made a salient move in his speech when he introduced his intention to revise the clause on denaturalization inscribed in the French civil code:

It should be possible to withdraw the French nationality from any person of foreign origin who has deliberately attempted to take the life of a police officer or of a member of the military police, or of any other representative of a public authority. French nationality must be earned, and one must demonstrate one's self to be worthy of it. When one shoots at a public authority agent, one is no longer worthy of being French. (2010, 16:50)

Here, Sarkozy's language further emphasizes the conflation of immigration with criminality through the specific identification of "any person of foreign origin." At the same time, his statement also works to enfold this identification within the notions of nation and nationality. Departing from a formal approach according to which national identity is seen as a set of facts linking an individual with the state (such as filiation, birth, schooling, residency, or military service) (Lagarde 2011, 3), Sarkozy's speech invokes nationality as a highly subjective and affective notion. According to him, national identity is a reward for a particular type of behavior that renders one "worthy" of it. He thereby focuses on the hierarchical dimension of national identity, emphasizing the personal ties of allegiance between an individual and the political power to which he or she is subjected. In this respect, Sarkozy's speech stages nationality as an individual and emotional investment from individuals to the state. Nationality is then viewed as a reward given by the state to individuals: it is granted on the basis of a distinctive apprehension of an individual's behavior and follows a predetermined set of performances.

It could be argued that this predetermined set of performances translates into the basic obligations bound to national citizenship rights. But even then, national citizenship cannot possibly be seen as a reward, as long as we accept that it remains a pivotal notion embedded in the notion of human rights inherited from the French Revolution and the corresponding endeavor to include every individual neutrally in a global system of law (Bauböck 1994, 236–39; Hirsch Ballin 2011, 26).

Furthermore, Sarkozy's intervention reveals that the term "reward" does not apply to each national citizen in the same way. First of all, the discourse maneuvers toward the establishment of specific power relations according to which French-born nationals are considered as hosts and new nationals as guests who must behave according to pre-established local rules. Second, and more importantly, Sarkozy's argument becomes incongruous when one realizes that the rule to which he refers—that is, one's obligation to respect the lives of public law enforcement representatives—is the most fundamental social and juridical rule applying to any and all residents of the Republic alike. It is safe to say that no country in the world grants any citizen the right to take the life of a public law enforcement officer. The former president's discursive trick is thus to ground his argument in a basic rule of conduct and to reiterate that same rule in terms of a particular law applying only to a subset of citizens. His discourse thereby appears logical and incontestable, while in fact it slyly creates a discursive shift that frames new nationals as threatening, generalized others.

Inhabiting the space of a politics of fear, denaturalization displaces the notion of security "as a practice of making 'enemy' and 'fear' the integrative, energetic principle of politics displacing the democratic principle of freedom and justice" (Huysmans 2014, 3). Furthermore, looking at denaturalization law involves analyzing a discourse that prefers the logic of state security to that of individuals; it means looking at a discourse that affects the safety of some citizens by placing them in physically or administratively precarious positions. While scholars have documented well the physical precariousness of detention centers where undocumented migrants must remain in humiliating conditions,[2] much less attention has been paid to the administrative precariousness stemming from practices of denaturalization. This is the juncture where this book intervenes. By focusing on denaturalization as a juridical concept and political tool, it shows the extent to which denaturalization practices have come to occupy a seminal place in politics of nationality and citizenship.

DENATURALIZATION AT THE CONVERGENCE OF NATIONALITY AND CITIZENSHIP

Since denaturalization operates at the convergence of nationality and citizenship, I sensed that finding out more about it would lead to a revised understanding of notions such as nationality and citizenship; I especially envisioned that knowing more about denaturalization would help to better understand current developments regarding the distribution (in terms of access and denial) of nationality and citizenship rights. Being among the most prominent institutions of our times, nationality and citizenship do not only regulate, as they do, the rights and obligations of people in a given state, but also their rights to movement into and across other states. At the same time, both nationality and citizenship are ambivalent forms of identification, as Sarkozy's Grenoble speech illustrates. To begin with, citizenship and nationality designate different forms of belonging and yet are often conflated.

Nationality first and foremost relates to nation-ness, which, as Benedict Anderson writes, is "the most universally legitimate value in the political life of our time" (2006, 3). Yet, concepts of nation, nationality, and nationalism "all have proved notoriously difficult to define, let alone to analyze" (3). The conceptual, epistemological, and philosophical studies available reflect the challenge posed by such a slippery object of study. Varying from an approach to the nation as spiritual community (Renan 1990) and studies that view the nation as an effect of industrialization (Gellner 2009) to yet another vision of nationhood that emphasizes the role of language in the construction of the nation as "imagined community" (Anderson 2006), the scholarly corpus on nations and national identities is particularly clear on one point: the image of the nation is, and must be, ambiguous, ambivalent, and Janus-faced (Balibar and Wallerstein 1991; Bhabha 1990; Nairn 1997).

Embedded in the juridical system of the nation-state, such ambivalence has never ceased to raise questions about who has the right to have rights, claim rights, or—as paradoxical as it might sound—be denied rights. On an immediate level, this question of one's access to rights brings questions of nationality and citizenship together, as the structure of the nation-state tends to conflate the one with the other. In a nation-state, citizenship rights most often include having the country's nationality and vice versa. But just as nationality, citizenship is a messy concept with multiple genealogies. For instance, some trace its origin to ancient Greece and predominantly refer to citizenship as a civic virtue at the service of the community, while others locate citizenship within a liberal framework, stressing individual rights and duties as primary concerns (Honohan 2017). But while individual rights have long been understood as a set of legal, political, and social rights (Marshall 1950), critical citizenship scholars have by now agreed that the scope of the rights associated with citizenship goes far beyond those three categories, as citizenship rights essentially include "the right to *claim* rights" in the first place (Isin 2012, 109, my emphasis). Viewed from this perspective, citizenship opens up beyond the restrictive idea of legal membership in the nation-state: for those denied legal rights at first, "the right to claim rights" highlights possibilities to be political despite formal, juridical restrictions (Isin 2002, 2012, 2017).

Weaving together questions of rights, identities, and security, notions of citizenship and nationality have become vectors of defining, challenging, and revising the boundaries of a political juridical community. Accordingly, both of the terms "nationality" and "citizenship" relate to questions of belonging, as much as to questions of repression. From the perspective of denaturalization, the terms "nationality" and "citizenship" are formative of the ways in which practices of repression play out as technologies of government, starting with the definition of what we perceive as social and political threats. It is those practices of defining what are perceived as social and political threats that are at the core of this book. More specifically, the book focuses on those mechanisms of exclusion that make use of citizenship and nationality as symbolic markers of repression.

JURIDICAL PARADOX AND THE TROPE OF SECURITY

The extent to which denaturalization practices rest on perceptions of social and political threats goes hand in hand with a loophole in the juridical expression of equality and security. In theory, and as expressed by François Héran

(2011), the notion of the (im)migrant is formally precluded from the French juridical lexicon. Article 1 of the Constitution—the text of reference *par excellence* in the overall national juridical structure—states that all French citizens are by definition fully equal before the law: "France ... shall ensure the equality of all citizens before the law, without distinction of origin, race or religion" (France 1958). A straightforward interpretation of this article is that migrants who have become French citizens have exactly the same status as every other French national. Accordingly, the notion of the (im)migrant citizen would remain a mere statistical and informal notion, that is, a notion independent of the formalities bound to French nationality (Héran 2011). Such a strict, constitutional approach to French nationality and citizenship fits the French republican concept of equality and reflects the ideal according to which a people form a national community because they live together in a bordered space, and not necessarily because they share the same history.

Looking at denaturalization, however, forces one to ask what is hiding behind the formal narrative of equality before the law. As the 2010 Sarkozy speech in Grenoble illustrates, equality assumes an Orwellian shape as it seems to imply that "all [people] are equal, but some [people] are more equal than others" (Orwell 1989, 97). This is not only true when analyzing the ways in which Sarkozy appropriated denaturalization in his discourse on the theme of fighting insecurity; the principle of equality before the law is also challenged by the legal article pertaining to denaturalization, article 25 of the French civil code on national identity.

Article 25 of the French civil code on national identity acknowledges situations in which the state has the ability to deprive naturalized nationals of their nationality. Its opening reads: "The individual who has acquired French nationality may, by order with the assent of the *Conseil d'État* (Supreme Court), be deprived of that nationality, unless denaturalization results in making him [*sic*] stateless" (France 1998). The article explicitly circumscribes its potential subjects as "nationals-by-acquisition." Consequently, talking about denaturalization requires one to distinguish "new" nationals from "French-born" nationals. In effect, article 25 thus asserts a distinction between (former) migrants and the rest of the citizenry.

As the language of denaturalization is solely addressed to those nationals who have acquired French nationality through immigration to France, it produces a discursive shift that cleaves open a space of struggle within the very concept of French national citizenship. It creates a new category of "citizen-migrant" that does not belong to the overall national juridical structure. Instead, denaturalization results in a specific form of irregular citizenship. In line with Peter Nyers's study on forms of irregular citizenship (2011), the concept of denaturalization becomes an expression of "contemporary processes of irregularization [that] contribute to wider processes by which the distinction of citizen/migrant becomes increasingly difficult to maintain. The logic of the 'secure citizen' vs. the 'dangerous migrant' is beginning to break down in both law and political practices" (187). In other words, the politics of denaturalization draws the category of the (national) citizen into practices of irregularization, which, carried out by state agents, participate in processes of making and unmaking citizenship. It is, accordingly, not sufficient to understand how "refugees, migrants, and temporary residents … [are] … made into irregular subjects. It is much more complex: citizens, too, are subject to irregularizing practices and attempts to make them into irregular subjects" (188). Studying denaturalization helps to understand the ways in which such irregularizing practices operate.

The first paragraph of article 25 of the French civil code further clarifies the possible conditions applying to denaturalization. It confirms that nationality becomes a differentiated concept when linked to security matters by stating that denaturalization can apply "if [the individual who has acquired French nationality] is guilty of an act which qualifies as an offense or a crime that undermines the fundamental interests of the Nation, or of a crime or offense constituting an act of terrorism" (France 1998). One can thus be denaturalized with reference to a criminal conviction for crimes that undermine the fundamental interests of the nation, or for terrorist acts. The reference to security is clear, as the vocabulary employed belongs to a lexical field of crime and punishment: "guilty," "offense" (two times), "crime" (two times), and "act of terrorism" are the main words in the paragraph. It is striking that all these words are relative: their meaning depends on a contextual and subjective interpretation. Accordingly, article 25 also performs through a high degree of contextual and subjective interpretation that generates an ambiguous discursive space. This ambiguous space is in itself performative, as it broadens denaturalization's potential field of operation. Not only is the notion of the migrant reinserted into juridical discourse, but the conditional parameters of its exceptional inscription are unclear and therefore potentially infinite.

The discursive ambiguity recurs in the phrase "fundamental interests of the nation" (as expressed in article 25 of the civil code) and its respective interpretations in the political debate. While Sarkozy appropriated it in terms of individual representatives of public forces, a parliamentary debate about denaturalization that followed Sarkozy's propositions suggested otherwise. As the opposition reminded the *Assemblée nationale* in the wake of Sarkozy's Grenoble speech in 2010, the primary interpretation of "fundamental interests of the nation" was initially meant to circumscribe acts of espionage and terrorism targeting the fundamental interests of the nation as a whole. So did Danièle Hoffman-Rispal, deputy of the opposition party SRC (Groupe Socialiste Républicain et Citoyen), as she observed that "[the] terrorist or the spy commits an act of war against his own society. He [*sic*] threatens its interests, its existential conditions, or directly attacks and undermines that existence. An attempt on the life of an individual is an act that is definitive and serious, which deserves the harshest sentences. However, it threatens neither the vital interests nor the life of the country" (France 2010). Hoffman-Rispal's comments aimed at clarifying the distinction between crimes committed against the vital interests of the state and crimes committed against individuals. Even though the latter are to be condemned and deserve the severest punishment applicable under criminal law, they do not belong, in any way, to the category of the former. It is precisely this distinction that was abolished in Sarkozy's Grenoble speech. The president blurred the notion of "nation" in terms of symbolic representation and symbolic institutions (instances of such symbolism would be the figure of the president as the representative of the whole nation, or the *Assemblée nationale* as a whole); he tweaked the term's definition so as to include individual representatives of public forces in the discursive circumscription of the term "nation."

Such discursive ambiguity has a particular effect: it turns denaturalization into a legal and political tool that reaches beyond the familiar opposition of national citizens versus foreigners. Denaturalization implies that immigrants (or even, by extension, children of immigrants) who have become French citizens are kept in a well-demarcated discursive space that frames them in terms of otherness and insecurity. Even when they have crossed the administrative border of national citizenship and have become French nationals, they remain segregated in the discursive field of immigration. While the language of denaturalization conveys that there is a group of French citizens who differ from other French citizens, the concept of nationality becomes a shared signifier for a plurality of signified entities. Native-born French nationals enjoy full citizenship and complete access to social and political rights, whereas new nationals are prevented from genuinely crossing the border between the field of foreignness and that of national citizenship; juridical-political interpretations of denaturalization keep them in the semantic field of otherness.

The legal and political interpretations at issue suggest that a discursive movement is taking place, which leads to a new juridical and administrative border no longer defined in terms of nationality or citizenship but rather in terms of a (distant) cultural otherness. It reflects those practices that Vivienne Jabri (2006) identifies as "a matrix of war," which she defines as "a set of diffuse practices, violence, disciplinary and control that at one and the same time target the other typified in cultural and racial terms and instantiate a wider remit of operations that impact upon society as a whole" (52). The aforementioned practices generate a process of racialization according to which individuals "can no longer simply be citizens of a secular, multicultural state, but are constituted in discourse as *particular citizens*, subjected to particular and hence exceptional practices" (53, my emphasis). They are also informed by a discourse of antagonism that eradicates any possibility of diversity within the profiled communities (53). This matches the working of denaturalization practices according to which former immigrants are constituted as particular citizens. Discursively speaking, their particularity translates into a political signifier that connects the internal logic of security to the political questions of cultural and racial identity (Huysmans 2000, 761). Eventually, it results in the precarious condition of their migrant identity—precarious in the sense that they belong to the ambiguous space of a structural, juridical, and potentially infinite exception.

A FOCUS ON LANGUAGE AND PERFORMATIVITY

When discursive ambiguities create new juridical political categories leading denaturalization practices to affect some citizens more than others, language becomes a seminal factor that influences people's lives and realities. J. L. Austin was one of the first to bring this active dimension of language to the attention of a wide audience with his seminal lecture series now known as *How to Do Things with Words* (1962). The main point in Austin's theory of language was to distinguish between descriptive and performative language. The point about performative language is that its content is not true or false. Instead, performative language acts to change our reality. As Jonathan Culler puts it, performative language is "acts of language that transform the world, bringing into being the things that they name" (2011, 97).

Since Austin's *How to Do Things with Words*, performativity has become a seminal concept in critical studies, leading to new interpretations of the term. Its relevance is most poetically rendered in Toni Morrison's (1993) words, "We die. That may be the meaning of life. But we do language. That may be the measure of our lives." We *do* language. We do language on a daily basis, and sometimes doing language simply amounts to using words to describe a situation. But if doing language is the measure of our lives, then surely it extends beyond merely describing a situation distant from us. Instead, doing language also involves acting with and through language. It means recognizing that language has agency: it is "an act with consequences," writes Judith Butler (1997, 6). In other words, viewing language as the measure of our lives is acknowledging that language is, in and of itself, political. It is political because it is something that we do together: we name, we recognize, we use codes and signs that are established over time and that only acquire meaning because of their repetition. And in those acts of naming, recognizing, coding, signing, and repeating, language becomes part of that which defines who we are.

At the crossroads of law and politics, practices of denaturalization are ensnared in layers of acts of language with consequences. The domain of the law is a specific context in which codes, signs, and categories are central. Politics, in turn, is a space of debate in which values and visions of rights and duties, justice and injustice, are being established and challenged. In between these domains, language travels like water. Trickling down administrative settings and formal boundaries, language connects the political with the juridical, the personal with the public, the rational with the affective. Flowing through and over boundaries, language charges itself with the qualities of the places and humans it traversed; it transports codes, meanings, and interpretations, which accumulate over time, like sediments. On the journey across disciplinary boundaries and across history, new meanings, codes, and signs emerge.

It is this journey of the language of denaturalization that I have followed in my research, with the aim of uncovering the measure of denaturalization practices. Accordingly, I have approached denaturalization through traces of linguistic representation, ranging from political discourses and debates on denaturalization to historical legislative texts with juridical comments, parliamentary documents, debates and reports, bills, decrees, and ministerial responses. Together, these documents developed a new narrative of national citizenship. Participating in the representation of the nation, they "[create] realities, discourses, images, fields of knowledge, and political contestation," while at the same time being "embedded in history, power relations, and current politics" (Peeren and Hoffmann 2010, 14). Considering my primary material as representations shifts attention from a mere authoritative reading to a reading that pays particular attention to the effects of language and the construction of meaning (Culler 2011, 62). I am less interested in what the texts were intended to convey than in how the texts work and what kind of truth they produce. This attention to denaturalization's politics of truth involves describing its nexus of "knowledge-power" in order to "grasp what constitutes the acceptability of [a system that legitimizes denaturalization practices]" (Foucault 2007b, 60–61). To do that, I concentrate on the narratives' textuality, by which I mean studying metaphors, rhetoric, and literary tropes as a way to unravel the performativity involved. In sum, paying attention to language and representation is a way to create a space for the primary sources to speak about the political force of the juridical language. The aim is to reveal the contingency involved when some values of sovereignty become institutionalized while others are suppressed.

MODES OF RESEARCH BETWEEN
GENEALOGY AND THE ARCHIVE

One of the main characteristics of denaturalization is its tendency to be hardly visible. Like water in a paper bag, it sometimes leaks into societal debates, yet it remains covered by an opaque layer of political and administrative justifications that claim to speak for themselves. Such quasi invisibility required specific modes of research. From a theoretical perspective, I found fertile grounds in a genealogical approach, as developed and adapted by a generation of scholars who have extended Foucault's understanding of genealogy in political philosophy, citizenship studies, security studies, and international relations (e.g., Brown 2001; Isin 2002; Aradau and Huysmans 2014). In line with my focus on language and performativity, genealogy is considered as a means to understand "politics out of history" (Brown 2001). While digging into the past to situate the present, genealogical research investigates moments when the meaning of an institutional norm (such as nationality or citizenship) was formed, contested, or revised. Accordingly, genealogical research especially investigates moments of ruptures and silences, with the aim to show "that some of our usually taken-for-granted ways of thinking about things are contingent products of messy history" (Koopman 2013, 145–46). By focusing on the contingency of norms, genealogy helps render the invisible visible in distribution patterns of power relations.

With regard to denaturalization, the juridical, political, and social categories that inform practices of denaturalization shed light on facets of nationality politics that have remained relatively unnamed: they reveal failures of national identity and citizenship, they disrupt and contest the dominant narratives on national citizenship produced so far, and they force us to reconsider what nationality and citizenship do to and with people. In other words, they invite us to rethink forms of political subjectivity. Not because denaturalization as such proposes alternative ways to think about rights and participation—it surely does not, its rationale being merely repressive, not creative. But studying denaturalization reveals a hidden rationality of our times. Writing and reading about denaturalization therefore becomes a tool to rethink those historical, cultural, social, and political categories that inform topical events and current social and political concerns. Denaturalization says much about cultural and political questions of belonging, and even more about the shifting boundaries of inclusion and exclusion.

From a practical perspective, doing genealogical research and digging into the past and the present involves archival research in the broad sense of the term. Depending on whether cases had been filed away in institutional archives or not, I have worked in national archives or have built my own archive of sources when working with contemporary cases. Following the theoretical insights of genealogy, my starting point was to identify moments of crisis in the history of France because moments of crisis *are* those moments when ruptures and silences cohabit in the noise of critical voices, social eruptions, and/or political takeovers. Wars, insurrections, and revolutions are indeed meaningful indicators of moments when seminal political and cultural concepts have been constructed, contested, or revised in contexts of insecurity. Focusing on those processes that legitimize denaturalization as a measure of repression, I have selected four main crises in the history of France: the French Revolution and its aftermath, World War I, World War II, and the inter-millennium decennia when the term "terrorism" gained prominence. The cases I have selected are cases that reveal the failures of the concepts of nationality and citizenship. In other words, what I especially looked for when digging into those moments of crisis were liminal cases, that is, cases that come in the place of the usual suspects. For instance, many would expect a case study on the place of foreigners during the project of the French Revolution but not so many would expect one on Olympe de Gouges. Yet precisely because Olympe de Gouges is usually not studied from the perspective of citizenship, her case offers an opportunity to view the concept of citizenship from new perspectives—that of affective citizenship in particular. Her case, then, enters a discursive space where the meaning of citizenship failed while at the same time being negotiated and instituted. The same is true, in a variety of shades, for all the cases that lead the analysis.

While this book focuses on denaturalization practices in continental France, there is room for further research, in particular around the intrinsic colonial aspect of norms of nationality and citizenship. Although colonialism is introduced as part of the analysis of the French revolutionary period and its aftermath, I have made the choice to not further address here denaturalization as used during the decolonization process, including the Algerian war and its aftermath, because much more in-depth research would be needed to properly disentangle the genealogies of imperial citizenship and the colonial difference. There is no doubt, however, that such research would raise fundamental questions about the validity of current ideas of nationality and citizenship, and deepen our understanding of how affective citizenship works as a technology of government. The colonial difference is a fundamental aspect of how norms of nationality and citizenship performed in the past and continue to perform today.

Based on past and present histories of denaturalization in the French nation, the narrative in this book develops an ever-changing image of those perceived as a threat to national security. Interrupting dominant understandings of nationality and citizenship, it exposes how the language of denaturalization interweaves concerns about immigration and national security; most of all, it presents national citizenship as a form of formal legal attachment and as a mode of emotional belonging.

Part I explores the French Revolution and its aftermath, a period during which the citizen became the central social, political, and juridical figure, leading the path to organize France as a nation. Although denaturalization as such did not exist yet, the analysis investigates those social, political, and juridical narratives through which the terms of citizenship performed within the emerging French nation. What interested me most was to find traces of the ways in which the institution of citizenship was established, contested, and revised, with the aim of gauging mechanisms of belonging and repression upstream of denaturalization practices.

Chapter 1 stages a theoretical discussion centered on the French Revolution as a producer of narratives about citizenship. Although historians and revolutionaries have turned the French Revolution into a key moment in the establishment of the modern notion of citizenship, the chapter invites us to question those dominant narratives and to look instead at the power relations they conceal. This first theoretical chapter is followed by four main case studies that manifest various modes of becoming foreign to the revolutionary ideals; they provide the backbones to research the limits of the universal model that had announced the citizen as the new political subject.

Chapter 2 examines the work done by territoriality as a concept and political tool that instigates mechanisms of inclusion and exclusion during the Revolution. Focusing on the categorizing and classifying principles of the law, the chapter addresses the development of a special police force controlling citizens of foreign origins. The administrative practices such as passport issuance, census taking, and the mandatory registration of newcomers' domiciles announced the beginning of a political thought centered on the notion of national identity in its territorial form. Were such practices a mere exception to the universal norm? Can we consider them as excesses of the dominant revolutionary discourse? To answer these questions, the chapter evaluates scholarly research concerning the increasing control of foreigners before proceeding to analyze the particular case of Mr. Scholler, a man of foreign origin who was arrested on French territory in 1793 and deported on the basis of his foreignness. Scholler's case offers primary material to assess the territorial and administrative logic at work in policing technologies of government; it emphasizes the preemptive and affective character of administrative security measures, and stresses territoriality as a determinant actor in technologies of governing borders and identities.

Chapter 3 further investigates the affective limits of universality in the dominant revolutionary discourse. It explores the case of Olympe de Gouges's trial in 1793, where the Revolutionary Court's interpretation of "love for the *patrie*" distinctively shaped the limits of citizenship. De Gouges's place in the history of citizenship is a particular one: denied citizen rights as a woman in a time when citizenship was reserved for men, she was formally excluded from the category of citizenship, but was nonetheless tried as a citizen who had put the revolutionary project at risk. Her case, then, enters a discursive space where the meaning of citizenship failed, while at the same time being negotiated and instituted. That she was denied citizenship, that she herself claimed citizen rights by mingling with the political quest of the Revolution, and that her death followed from her political engagement all invite consideration of her trial as an expression of the political struggles in and of the establishment of citizenship.

Finally, chapter 4 examines the work done by the new juridical norms in defining the contours of France's political community. First discussing the 1848 decree on the abolition of slavery, in which citizenship is exposed as an administrative moral code, the chapter highlights the peculiar contrast between the punishment inflicted upon citizens still trading in slavery and those punishments inflicted upon slaves who disobeyed their masters. Citizens who traded in slavery or owned slaves lost their citizenship, while slaves who disobeyed their masters were put to death. Looking at the difference in technologies of government concerning the production of political subjectivity and the denial thereof, the chapter advances the argument that juridical political frames of recognition made the colonial subject decidedly more difficult to recognize as full political subject. For instance, although the abolition decree formally freed slaves from forced labor, slaves were still caught in a social, political, and juridical infrastructure that was primarily beneficial to the white male bourgeoisie while it continued to de-civilize, brutalize, and degrade colonized people (Césaire 1972, 2). Furthermore, the case of Mr. Furcy, who challenged norms of recognition in justice so as to gain his freedom as a man and as a citizen, emphasizes dynamics of belonging and repression constitutive of France's political juridical community.

Part II further addresses denaturalization as a technology of government in times of war. The chapters are divided between World War I and World War II and highlight how politics of denaturalization contributed to model a performative image of a national self. At the same time, politics of denaturalization helped define and create strangers across various registers: from spies during World War I, to communists in the 1930s, to Jews and political dissidents during World War II. Based on parliamentary documents, juridical texts, and expert commentaries, the chapters pay particular attention to the rhetoric and literary tropes produced by those juridical and political texts. For instance, a frequent metaphor represents the nation as a family, with French-born nationals as the children of the *patrie*. Such logic of nativism both entertains a structural suspicion against (former) migrants, and betrays a politics of nationality that structurally prioritizes those born as French nationals, thereby raising questions about what it means to belong and about the place of nationality and citizenship in governmental technologies of repression.

Chapter 5 focuses on the consequences of the first denaturalization law in France, promulgated in April 1915. The analysis demonstrates that the language of denaturalization operates as an instrumental logic to maintain and secure the national community as it stems from security and emergency rhetoric. Denaturalization gave the state the possibility of taking away someone's French nationality if that person was born in an enemy nation. Denaturalization was thus primarily meant as an exceptional law, during the war, to deal with spying activities. Article 7 of this first law explicitly stated that the law would cease to be enforceable two years after peace was definitively signed. What the history of denaturalization demonstrates, however, is that it is easier to promulgate a law than to abrogate it; it shows the extent to which, once at work in the French civil code on nationality, the language of denaturalization began to perform. Denaturalization had become part of the vocabulary of nationality, gaining performativity as it gained historicity.

After having demonstrated the power of affect in the context of World War I, the chapters focusing on World War II (chapter 6 and 7) further devote attention to the significance of knowledge politics. Despite the multitude of research, studies, and debates concerning the time frame of the war, very little remains known about denaturalization practices before, during, and after the war, in France and Europe. For instance, most French people remain unaware of de Gaulle's *déchéance* while he was leading the Free France resistance movement from London. This prompts the following question: What would it do to the French conception of nationality if every French child were to learn in school about de Gaulle's denaturalization? And in retrospect, what does it do to us to realize that de Gaulle lost his nationality while, at the same, gaining such a position in the Resistance that, after the war, his presidency came as no surprise? Accordingly, in the name of which community does a denaturalization decree become authorized? Based on material collected in the French National Archives, the analysis of World War II reviews three political strategies in which denaturalization played a prominent role: chapter 6 discusses the extension of denaturalization practices in the prewar period; chapter 7 explores the systematic revision of naturalization decrees during the war, as well as the *dégradation nationale* [sentence of civic degradation] in the postwar period. While all three cases emphasize the adaptability of the law when governments aim to maintain a certain form of the national community, the analysis stresses the programmatic and normative force of the concept of nationality that turns the very concept of national citizenship into a mobile yet limitative notion.

Part III further addresses the problematic adaptability of the law and its relation to the definition of who must be seen as a threatening subject. Where the analysis of World War II politics provides an account of what happens when the adaptability of the law expands to such an extent that its contours drift into illegitimate grounds, Part III analyzes the effect of such adaptability when ambiguous legal categories have become a common and legitimized feature of contemporary counterterrorism measures.

Chapter 8 retraces the historical trajectories according to which the notion of terrorism has been inscribed in the law, and in the law on denaturalization in particular; it discusses the extent to which "terrorism," as a concept that lacks definite semantic content, has become an incantatory term that justifies and legitimizes practices of denaturalization. Surveying a selection of parliamentary debates and parliamentary documents pertaining to the latest amendment to article 25 of the civil code on national identity, discussed and adopted in the context of the fight against terrorism in France beginning in the 1980s, the analysis reveals the rhetorical and political aberrations that led to the inclusion of the word "terrorism" in the juridical norm of denaturalization. The chapter further analyzes the political deliberations leading to the juridical definition of terrorism in the late 1980s. It highlights the tension between the notorious difficulty to define the term in the first place, as expressed in one of the rapporteurs' expression *introuvable définition* [missing/unknown definition] and a political will to define terrorism so as to be able to punish terrorists accordingly.

Chapter 9 reports on the most recent developments in terms of denaturalization legislation, exposing the significance of the French case beyond France. While discussing the place of denaturalization in contemporary and (inter)national politics of security, the chapter emphasizes the extent to which the security crisis represents a test for politics of national citizenship. The resignation of former minister of justice Christiane Taubira, who resigned in 2016 over the government's proposition to include measures of denaturalization in the French Constitution, demonstrates that the stakes are high. In the context of national and global insecurity, the political will to denaturalize those deemed a fundamental threat starts to openly challenge fundamental democratic and republican principles. The governmental proposition was not only to insert denaturalization measures in the Constitution; it was also to broaden denaturalization measures to all French nationals deemed a fundamental threat to the nation, thereby spreading the totalitarian infection deeper. While the deprivation of rights appears as an answer to collective fear, the chapter argues that the language of denaturalization turns those persons who are prosecuted in the name of the state's security into foreigners. It literally makes foreign those being prosecuted through empirically defined administrative categories (e.g., national citizenship); it conflates concerns about immigration with security issues; and most importantly, denaturalization makes foreign those who are constructed as a threat beyond any empirical line. It is used for political purposes, emphasizing the relativity of the principle of equality as it enables governments to review, adapt, and rework the definition of the "threatening" subject.

Finally, the conclusion reflects back on the genealogical trajectory of the book and underlines the affective constitution of denaturalization as a technology of government.

NOTES

1. The conflation of immigration law with criminal law has even resulted in an area of scholarly research on "crimmigration," that is, "the convergence of immigration and criminal law" (Stumpf 2006, 366). The term "crimmigration" originated in US-American literature on illegal immigration and security issues (e.g., Stumpf 2006) and has now entered, for instance, Dutch scholarly literature of the same theme (e.g., Leun 2010). In October 2012, a crimmigration conference took place in Coimbra, Portugal, indicating a growing scholarly interest in the topic. In my view, the term is inadequate as it intuitively insinuates that immigration itself is understood as criminal; the term thereby adds up to the discursive convergence of immigration and criminal law and fails to address the problem critically. Nonetheless, the term's aim to target the criminalization of immigration *through state policies* remains compelling and highly relevant in a context where immigration and criminality are almost systematically presented as one and the same thing.

2. A sample of relevant authors and titles on the topic of the precariousness of states of exception, asylum, and detention are Hannah Arendt's *The Origins of Totalitarianism* (1973); Giorgio Agamben's *Homo Sacer: Sovereign Power and Bare Life* (1998); Étienne Balibar's *Droit de Cité* (1998) and *We, the People of Europe?* (2004); Seyla Benhabib's *The Rights of Others: Aliens Residents and Citizens* (2004) and Benhabib and Robert Post's *Another Cosmopolitanism* (2006); Gérard Noiriel's *Réfugiés et Sans Papiers* (1998); Peter Nyers's "Abject Cosmopolitanism: The Politics of Protection in the Anti-Deportation Movement" (2003) and "In Solitary, in Solidarity: Detainees, Hostages and Contesting the Anti-Policy of Detention" (2008); David Farrier's *Postcolonial Asylum: Seeking Sanctuary Before the Law* (2011) (which gives a rich overview of the literature on the topic of asylum and its precarious conditions). Moreover, scholarly journals such as the *Journal of Refugee Studies*, *Borderlands*, and *Journal of Immigration, Asylum and Nationality Law* (to name just a few) reflect the broad approach to the topic in scholarly literature.

Part I

THE FOREIGNER OF THE FRENCH REVOLUTION

Chapter 1

The French Revolution

A Producer of Narratives about Citizenship

The events of the 1789 French Revolution led to radical changes in the organization of France. When the royal family was deposed, its sovereign power was replaced by new ruling republican elites who claimed to represent the people at large through an *Assemblée*. Claiming that a republican institution would guarantee the rights of the people—as opposed to a ruling and hereditary monarchy—the republican elites developed a new political framework based on the philosophical ideas of the Enlightenment. Central to these ideas was the notion of "nation," a social and political concept that was primarily connected to the idea of an emancipatory liberty, be it from colonial, aristocratic, or imperial power (Noiriel 2005, 135). As a social and political organ, the nation essentially emerged in relation to a broader social protest that raised questions of identity in the process of defining whose sovereign power the nation would—or should—represent (135–36). According to Gérard Noiriel, the emergence of the nation involved a discursive construction of the nation's identity according to which the nation itself became increasingly personified, causing its identity to be defined on a twofold basis (136). On the one hand, it expressed its uniqueness by displaying its objective identity in opposition to others (136). On the other, it also developed a subjective identity, that is, an identity based on a supposed development through time, characterized by memory or by the presence of its own past in its present (136). The nation became a complex organ that played a major role in the development of new political ideas, while its form and agency still needed to be socially, politically, and juridically defined.

Along with the development of the nation and its identity, a new form of political subjectivity was born: the citizen. Primarily narrated through the Declaration of the Rights of Man and of the Citizen (1789), the citizen was installed as the new omnipresent political subject. This is not to say that the

concept of the citizen itself was invented during the French Revolution. Engin
Isin (2002) has shown in meticulous detail that the notion of citizenship
long preceded the French Revolution. He explains that "every age since the
ancient Greeks fashioned an image of being political based upon citizenship"
(1). Accordingly, instead of having invented the notion of the citizen, French
revolutionaries appropriated specific images of citizenship from earlier soci-
eties, such as the Greek *polis* and the Roman *civitas* (121). Nonetheless,
revolutionary narratives did claim a specific image of the revolutionary event
according to which the new democratic government—made by and for citizens—was differentiated from cities as governing bodies. Specifically, they
created a new, dominant image of the citizen around which an entire social,
political, and juridical structure was to be constructed. Modern historians
have tended to reproduce those narratives without critically assessing for
what purposes those specific images of citizenship were mobilized at that
specific time (Isin 2002, 121). By doing so, both historians and revolutionaries have turned the French Revolution into a key moment in the establishment of the modern notion of citizenship.

Throughout *Being Political: Genealogies of Citizenship* (2002), Isin invites
us to question these dominant narratives, "not because they give us false or
implausible images, but because we must understand for what purposes or
uses these images were mobilized" (121). In a similar vein, this genealogy of
denaturalization law in France aims to further investigate, in a first stage, the
various imaginaries informing the revolutionary understanding of citizenship.
Focusing on the late eighteenth- and early nineteenth-century political and
juridical narratives, it recognizes a transition with respect to forms of political agency. As producers of narratives, the revolutionaries crystallized their
understanding of citizenship in texts meant to sustain the new political and
juridical system.[1] To the extent that they reshaped the reality of the political
subject around the notion of citizenship inscribed into the frame of the nation,
such revolutionary narratives are meaningful instances of performative language; they contributed to the realization of a new social, political, and juridical system, thereby becoming acts with consequences. As such, they defined
new modes of recognition, including new lines of belonging and repression.

Such contextual framework leads to the following questions: In which
specific terms did the revolutionary narratives address individual subjects?
What is the relationship between subject and citizen, and how did it relate to
the emergence of the notion of national identity? And finally, what do these
narratives tell us about the production of a "threatening otherness" along the
lines of national identity, citizenship, and security discourses?

CITIZEN SUBJECT AND SUBJECT CITIZEN: WHO COMES AFTER THE SUBJECT?

Investigating the concept of the citizen during the French Revolution, Étienne Balibar's essay, entitled "Citizen Subject" (1991), helps us to understand what is at stake when we consider the citizen as a new modern political subject. His essay responds to Jean-Luc Nancy's question of "Who comes after the subject?" (Cadava, Connor, and Nancy 1991). Although leading to a large philosophical discussion, Balibar's primary answer is wonderfully concise: "After the subject comes the citizen," he says (38).

Balibar's answer, significantly, is placed in the context of the French Revolution, with 1789 marked as a moment of irreversibility, in other words, as "the effect of a rupture" in what he calls the "process of the substitution of the citizen for the subject" (1991, 39). This is not to say that Balibar dismisses earlier origins of the notion of citizenship.[2] Instead, his argument merely maintains that the French Revolution—and the year 1789 in particular—produced a rupture in the evolution of the term (44). This rupture is predominantly connected to the fact that the revolutionary system of law defined the subject as citizen, while the citizen reciprocally defined the system of law. The effect of such a reciprocal definition is that the revolutionary event faced a moment of irreversibility: the citizen had become both the one who received the quality of being a citizen and the one who decided on the parameters of what a citizen can, or should be. In other words, the citizen needed to comply with the rules of what it meant to be a citizen while at the same time having control over the definition of those rules.

However, if the citizen comes after the subject, this raises the question of who was the subject, and how might he or she genuinely relate to the citizen? The *who* question is crucial, Balibar notes, because it implies an interpretation of the subject that, while it defines a new origin, can neither be the origin of the subject nor that of the citizen "because the origin *is not* the subject, but man" (1991, 39).

The idea of *man* thought of as the origin of both subject and citizen is a seminal feature of revolutionary narratives. As Hannah Arendt (1990, 108) puts it, "[revolutionaries] believed that they had emancipated nature herself, as it were, liberated the natural man in all men, and given him the Rights of Man to which each was entitled, not by virtue of the body politics to which he belonged but by virtue of being born." Indeed, when reading the text of the Declaration of the Rights of Man and of the Citizen, it becomes evident that *man* remains central to the new political and juridical narrative. Moreover, we can observe that the dominant revolutionary discourse is fully grounded in the twofold basis of law and nature: while working on establishing a system of law that had to be potentially universal in its reach, Revolutionaries considered human nature as the primary defining basis of their claim to a universal system. In other words, nature prefigured institutions while being defined by them (Thomas 2011, 27).

Such mutually constitutive dynamic between nature and institutions is most saliently present in the first two articles of the Declaration of the Rights of Man, which read:

> Article I
>   Men are born and remain free and equal in rights. Social distinctions may be founded only upon the general good.
> Article II
>   The aim of all political association is the preservation of the natural and imprescriptible rights of man. These rights are liberty, property, security, and resistance to oppression.[3]

As Jacques Rancière observes (2004, 300), in these articles, "[t]he Rights of Man make natural life appear as the source and the bearer of rights. They make birth appear as the principle of sovereignty." Identifying birth as the fundamental principle of sovereignty has consequences for appreciating the substitution of the citizen for the subject. Indeed, by referring to birth as a defining moment in the enactment of the rights of man ("people *are born* free and equal in rights"), the revolutionary text reaffirms the natural origin of the subject while affording it juridical and political clothing in terms of citizenship. Similarly, Balibar (1991, 44) points out that the duality of man and citizen holds the possibility of an antithetical reading: Is it *man* or *citizen* that is the founding notion of the Declaration? Are the rights those of the citizen *as man*, or those of the man *as citizen* (44)?

Balibar initially confirms that the Declaration had indeed established the rights of man *as citizen*, because "the stated rights are those of the citizen, the objective is the constitution of citizenship" (1991, 44). In contrast, Rancière's (2004) reading further emphasizes the antithetical movement embedded in the enunciation of those rights and seems to privilege a reading of the Rights of Man as the rights of the citizen *as man*. Indeed, by labeling the rights of man as "natural and imprescriptible rights," the second article of the Declaration accentuates the natural quality that constitutes the juridical notion of the citizen; it reasserts the semi-equation between man and citizen already enunciated in its title. Yet, whereas the title of the Declaration leaves the equation open by means of the connective "and," the content of the articles suggests that the function of the connective is to assimilate "man" with "citizen." In that respect, each reading of the Declaration inevitably reiterates the antithetical movement discussed above. Its enunciation of the rights of man *as citizen* depends on a definition of the citizen *as man*. In Balibar's (1991, 45) words, "the citizen is a man in enjoyment of all his 'natural' rights, completely realizing his individual humanity, a free man simply because he is equal to every other man." Hence, the citizen is always—and by definition—a *supposed subject* (i.e., a legal subject, psychological subject, or transcendental subject) (45).

Accordingly, while citizens' rights are defined for the citizen *as man*, the citizen itself is caught in a process of becoming a subject (Balibar 1991, 45). Therefore, the universal claim of the revolutionary system of law is precisely based on a consideration of the citizen-subject understood through the humanity of man (i.e., the natural origin of the subject), thereby typically performing the mechanism of juridical fiction according to which the law announces its juridical propositions "as if" it were reality.[4]

FROM UNIVERSAL LANGUAGE TO MODES OF BELONGING AND REPRESSION

Sophie Wahnich's (2010a) analysis of the revolutionary period provides useful material to further discuss the ways in which the newly defined political and juridical structure had been naturalized. Focusing on the shift taking place at the level of identification practices, Wahnich equates the new *national* mode of identification with what she terms a "new organic solidarity" (56). Such natural labeling both contrasts and competes with earlier forms of local identification practices, which she expresses in terms of a "mechanical solidarity of the villages" (56). According to Wahnich, the formation of the national—hence specific—community thus went along with a naturalized appreciation of the community. In other words, while the boundaries of the nation were set up in terms of a social and political community, the relational mode of the national population was defined on the basis of an organic, universal condition of being.

This dynamic between the social political realm and the naturalized appreciation of social political relations typically reflects the ambiguous statements of the Declaration. Standing in as a national narrative instigated by the revolutionaries, the Declaration needed to be interpreted both in terms of its political and juridical specificity, and in terms of the universal condition of being. Furthermore, this dynamic confirms that it is primarily the narrated integration of the notion of birth—as opposed to the concepts of Liberty, Equality, and Fraternity—that sustains the sole imaginable universal dimension of the revolutionary discourse. Hence, based on the notion of birth, the Declaration of the Rights of Man and of the Citizen endeavors to expand the—incommensurable—moment of universality to a generalized social, political, and juridical code. Accordingly, each newly born human being is governed by the discourse of the law that pretends to construct them as independent of that law. The inevitable categories of the juridical system, however, necessarily prevent the further application of birth in its universal dimension; by definition, the discourse of the law shapes a set of distinctions and hierarchies, thereby forming lines of belonging and repression.

The creator of a political and juridical structure, the revolutionary discourse was thus caught in its own categorizing and classifying principle, thereby drifting away from its universal ideal. On the one side, it claimed that it suffices to be born to become a citizen; on the other, the juridical discourse was based on a set of conditions that restricted the access to citizenship, constructing categories of foreignness that came to be opposed to the notion of the citizen. In other words, birth alone was no longer sufficient to become a citizen. Instead, one had to comply with a set of conditions, which were, however, silenced by the vocabulary of the universal employed in and by the law.

Arendt's analysis of the French Revolution in the social political context of what she calls "the conquest of the state by the nation" (1973, 230) provides a meaningful additional layer to further understand what was at stake in this dynamic between universal language and the particular conditions of juridical terms. More specifically, Arendt's analysis helps further specify the terms in which the revolutionary narratives shifted from universal language to modes of belonging and repression. According to Arendt, the particular, differentiating quality of the juridical system during the French Revolution was especially a consequence of the nation becoming associated with the state, thereby forming a nation-state (229). Such association between state and nation was characteristic of the French Revolution, says Arendt (229), and had far-reaching consequences. In Beiner's (2000, 50) words, "the pairing of the state with the nation [set] in motion a dialectic whose eventual outcome [was] the destruction of the state as a moral-juridical shelter for its citizens."

The value of Arendt's perception of the Revolution is thus in zooming into the dynamic between the idea of nation and the state structure. According to her, the state was likely to realize the universal potential of the Revolution because "[whether] in the form of a new republic or of a reformed constitutional monarchy, the state inherited as its supreme function the protection of all inhabitants in its territory no matter what their nationality, and was supposed to act as a supreme legal institution" (1973, 230). But as the state was paired with the upcoming idea of nation, the nation's naturalized understanding of social relations started to shift from a universal perspective on rights and protection to a particular one. As she puts it, "The tragedy of the nation-state was that the people's rising national consciousness interfered with [the state's supreme function of protection]" (230). Such interference provoked the so-called *universal* rights of man to become particular, national rights (230–32); the romantic representation of a "national soul" was substituted for the states' conception of popular representation (231); and nationalism became "the expression of this perversion of the state into an instrument of the nation" (231). As Beiner (2000, 50) explains it, nationalism therefore became "a pathology of citizenship that, having subordinated the state to the idea of the nation, [generated] a further pathology in a more expansionary notion of nationhood surpassing the boundaries (and therefore the moral limits) of the state."

Concerning denaturalization, Arendt's notion of the conquest of the state by the nation raises the question as to whether denaturalization might indeed be one of these technologies of government through which the nation has succeeded in conquering the state. Since denaturalization practices express the limits of norms of belonging and activate criteria of repression within the nation-state, they make visible which set of conditions restricts the access to citizenship while constructing categories of foreignness. While enacting moments when citizen rights prove indeed to be alienable, denaturalization practices are acts that tear open the veil of universal terms at work in the republican ideal of the universal rights of man and of the citizen.

In order to better grasp which particular conditions have challenged and revised the initially universal conception of citizenship, the following three chapters each delve into a specific instance when norms of belonging and repression were established, contested and/or revised during and after the Revolution; more specifically, they explore the ways in which the nation-state constructs specific norms of belonging while activating repressive criteria. While each of the upcoming cases sheds light on denaturalization as a technology of government by mapping out mechanisms of belonging and repression constitutive of the French nation, the aim is not to draw a linear sequencing or causal connections between the cases and periods presented. Instead, following a genealogical gesture, the aim is to show that together, these cases express the extent to which revolutionary narratives came to justify extreme measures of exclusion in the name of the law, the latter being caught up in the misleading vocabulary of the universal. Thus, each case illustrates the limits of the revolutionary universal project as they reveal the specific categories that came to be superimposed on the primary universal condition of being born, hence defining processes of becoming estranged from the revolutionary system.

NOTES

1. One of those was the Declaration of the Rights of Man and of the Citizen of 1789, which marked a defining moment in the formation of the new social, political and juridical system and has remained a key reference ever since.

2. Many of Balibar's writings give an account of the broader genealogies of the concept of citizenship. See "Propositions on Citizenship" (1988) and *We, the People of Europe?* (Balibar and Swenson 2004).

3. Translation: *The Avalon Project: Documents in Law, History and Diplomacy* ("Avalon Project—Declaration of the Rights of Man—1789," 2018).

4. For further references on the law as being an imaginary and fictive principle, I refer the reader to Foucault's lecture series *Security, Territory and Population* (2007a), specifically the January 18, 1978, lecture on the general features of apparatuses of security, in which he discusses the main differences between apparatuses of security and disciplinary mechanisms, taking the law as one of the central elements. Derrida's arguments in *Of Hospitality* (Derrida and Dufourmantelle 2000), as well as his discussion of the deconstructable essence of the structure of law in "Force of Law" (Derrida 1990), are also relevant to the discussion. Likewise, Thomas's chapter "Fictio legis" in *Les Operations du droit* (2011) as well as Simonin's *Le Déshonneur dans la République* (2008) (esp. pages 277–84) and her take on the revolutionary period discussed in Calafat's article "Droit pénal et état d'exception" (2011) provide further insights into the question.

Chapter 2

Becoming Foreign 1

The Nation as Space Susceptible to Intrusion

In theory, the formal function of the revolutionary law applied to everyone irrespective of one's place of birth or bloodline. It thereby created a political subject that solely needed to be born in order to have access to the political and juridical structure. In practice however, the system of law is by definition based on categorizing and classifying principles. Such principles contravene any possible universal claim, except perhaps in the context of the incommensurable moment of birth. Yet being integrated into the juridical discourse, the notion of birth performatively allowed the revolutionary legal narratives to signify that the category of the subject was indeed universal, as discussed in chapter 1.

Before long, however, the practical application of the juridical and political discourse problematized and dissolved the universal category of the citizen. For instance, administrative practices such as passport issuance, census taking, and the mandatory registration of newcomers' domiciles announced both the defeat of the Enlightenment ideal and the beginning of a political thought centered on the notion of national identity in its territorial form. Such a dynamic has been convincingly expressed by Wahnich (2010b, xiv) in the following terms:

> The battle is lost when the political category merges with the administrative and juridical category according to which every foreigner becomes *a-priori* a suspect. .... This categorical superimposition is one of the defeats of the Enlightenment ideal. It led to the rule that all civil servants must be French; and *in fine* to the notion of nationality which establishes a qualitative distinction between being French and being a citizen in year Thermidor II. Until then, the quality of a citizen was assessed politically without any reference to one's nationality. Many foreigners were considered to be good citizens.

The reality of administrative practices meant that in practice, it was no longer sufficient to simply be born in order to have access to the citizen category. Instead, the legal framework defining the surface of the administration body led to a first exception to its universal ideal: one had to be born *in the nation* in order to be able to fully participate in the revolutionary project.

Were such administrative practices a mere exception to the norm? Can we consider them as excesses of the revolutionary discourse?[1] In other words, could the revolutionary discourse still be granted a universal potential despite the impossibility for some to gain access to the rights promised to humanity as a whole? The chapter approaches these questions by first considering the development of a special police force charged with controlling citizens of foreign origin, which Wahnich (2010a) meticulously researched and described in *L'Impossible Citoyen*. While discussing the process of conflation that took place with regard to the administration of foreigners, the analysis introduces the term of "metonymic slide" in relation to what Sara Ahmed (2004a, 2004b) has identified as "affective economies," thereby revealing the performative dimension of administrative practices within which language and emotions cohabit as they shape the surface of the national community. Finally, the case of Mr. Scholler, a man of foreign origin who was arrested on French territory in 1793 and deported on the basis of his foreignness, helps further investigate the constitutive dynamics of administrative practices and territorial logics when mobilized in the name of communal safety.

FOREIGNNESS, TERRITORY, AND AFFECTIVE PREEMPTION

During the French Revolution, the term "foreigner" had no straightforward definition. Caught up between political and juridical perceptions, it referred to a wide pallet of behaviors, professions, or filiations. As Whanich (2010a) has identified, the figure of the foreigner was at first applied to the isolated man, the contra-revolutionary citizen, and the stateless mercenary (95).[2] In these three cases, the appellation "foreigner" was linked to a behavioral judgment, as when foreigners were associated with suspicious and condemnable conduct. Isolated men were seen as those who refused to take part in the social relationship formed by the revolutionary event (60). Their refusal was interpreted as an obstruction to the realization of the republican nation, which, by ways of its humanity, was meant to be one and indivisible (60). Contra-revolutionaries were by definition enemies of the people insofar as they did not support the revolutionary developments and thus belonged to those who needed to be defeated. As for stateless mercenaries, they were feared for their lack of attachment to the country and therefore suspected of enlisting in enemy armies (94).

What stands out is that the dyad foreigner/national revolved around the revolutionary premise that the nation must be one and indivisible (Wahnich 2010a, 81). Becoming a foreigner implied becoming an outsider, which implied belonging to the category of a national enemy who needed to be controlled and expelled from the territory. This is not to say, however, that the Revolution as a whole was a xenophobic enterprise. Many foreigners were in fact initially deemed good citizens and were able to participate in the revolutionary project (Wahnich 2010b, xiv; Rapport 2000). In 1790, the general trend was still to experience the law as the symbolic link between all sorts of differences in the name of humanity (Wahnich 2010a, 63). Differences in origins hence seemed to be irrelevant before the law, and all people of foreign origin could, in principle, become French citizens. Following this ideal, one was not a foreigner because of one's origin but because of one's refusal to subordinate one's particularities to the national unity (63). In other words, it was not so much one's origin that produced the mark of foreignness, but rather one's political behavior (92).

The revolutionary debate reveals, however, that the notion of citizenship was increasingly coupled with a nationalized approach to the political domain. From 1793 onward, following the logic of a state evolving toward the form of a *nation*-state, individuals born in one of the countries at war with France started to be categorized as suspects regardless of their individual political practices (Wahnich 2010a, 34, 81; Brubaker 1992, 46–47). Such focus on one's national origin in demarcating the trustworthy citizen from the threatening other went hand in hand with language becoming an increasingly important marker of identity. As Michael Rapport recapitulates in his study *Nationality and Citizenship in Revolutionary France* (2000, 13), "[the] surveillance, arrest, and expulsion of foreigners in the Terror occurred as the logical outcome of revolutionary ideology and language. In the case of foreigners, it was the product of the irreconcilable tension between universalism and the idea of the nation. The exclusion of foreigners was, above all, the result of nationality becoming the essential criterion for citizenship."

Such nationalized approach to the political domain emphasizes the concomitant performance of the terms of nation and safety, thereby increasingly embedding the discourse of nation and nationality into a territorialized perception of national boundaries. Not only did the nation start to conquer the universal potential of citizenship as a political subject (Arendt 1973, 230), but it also started to perform in the name of public safety. In Wahnich's terms, people of foreign origin began to be preemptively arrested and deported on the sole justification that they could be suspected of potential treason (2010a, 35).[3] Such preemptive practices were soon formalized in the form of a new law authorizing the expulsion of foreigners (97). Not only did the law require the expulsion of foreigners, but it also called for the expulsion of any person unable to justify their presence in the city as well as for a financial sanction or imprisonment of those offering them hospitality (98).[4] As Wahnich explains, those arrested who still claimed to be sympathetic to the Revolution were asked to become super-patriots by being able to understand, as no one else, the security measures being taken against them (35). This law was not a mere radicalization of former security measures, Wahnich argues, but rather proof of the profound transformations taking place around surveillance practices and emotions of suspicion (97). At this stage, the political foreigner became indistinguishable from the migrant foreigner (81).

This shift in perceptions of foreignness, which occurred in the late 1790s and led to the identification of migrants as a potential threat to the nation, significantly reflects that which Ahmed (2004b, 2004a) has described in terms of a metonymic slide. A metonymic slide is a movement between signs through which "the literal term of one thing is applied to another with which it has become closely associated because of a recurrent relationship in common experience" (Abrams 1999, 99). Although the concept of metonymy is most common in literary studies, Ahmed has persuasively shown that its mechanisms are usefully relevant for analyzing processes of identity and community formation. Informed by an interdisciplinary framework at the crossroads of gender studies and postcolonial theory, her understanding of metonymic slide takes shape throughout her theories of affective economies, and is centered on the discursive and performative dynamic of nation-states. More specifically, the term addresses those familiar narratives (such as political rhetoric or media-driven stories) in which particular subjects, such as immigrants or asylum seekers, are positioned as a threat to the collective body. Especially focused on the directions and movements of collective emotions, Ahmed posits that metonymic slides shape surfaces of collective bodies. According to her, "[the] movement between signs is what allows others to be attributed with emotional value, … as being fearsome" (2004a, 127). While "the individual subject comes into being through its very alignment with the collective" (128), "emotions are not 'in' either the individual or the social, but produce the very surfaces and boundaries that allow the individual and the social to be delineated as if they are objects" (2004b, 10). On the one hand, metonymic slides are the technical discursive mechanism giving shape to such social alignments; on the other, emotions are never fixed. Instead, the movement between signs occurs thanks to the presence of an empty discursive space where the void allows the circulation of emotions, making room for signs to move.

Ahmed's thesis of affective economies was specifically developed in reference to the racialization of criminality in contemporary debates on immigration, but her observations help understand what was at stake in the revolutionary surveillance practices. Referring to the vocabulary of threat and violence employed by politicians while discussing issues of immigration,[5] Ahmed (2004a, 127) notices that "[through] the circulation of signs of fear, the black other 'becomes' fearsome." Translated into the context of the revolutionary discourse and its surveillance practices in particular, it can now be stated that those of foreign origin became suspect through the circulation of signs of suspicion. Designating the political foreigner *and* the one of foreign origin, the sign of "foreigner" became a shared signifier for both contra-revolutionaries and newcomers.

According to Ahmed (2004a, 127), such metonymic gestures go hand in hand with the circulation and accumulation of emotions between signs and specific bodies. Emotions, such as fear or suspicion, do not remain within words, nor do they fully transfer from linguistic signs into bodily sensations. Instead, emotions circulate between the realm of language and the bodies of those being designated by the linguistic categories involved. As performative particles of the matter that constitutes the link between linguistic signs and our physical reality, emotions flow between signs and bodies, leaving sedimentary traces behind. The more they circulate, the more traces build up, forming, as they swirl, a defining boundary between the self and the other.

Moreover, in such process of linguistic and emotional sedimentation, emotions such as fear "[do] not reside in a particular object or sign, and it is this lack of residence that allows [them] to slide across signs, and between bodies" (Ahmed 2004a, 127). For instance, emotions of suspicion toward foreigners "do not have a fixed referent" (123); there is no particular object of fear, but instead an administrative, general, *and* linguistic association that brings the terms of "foreigner" and "insecurity" together. But it is precisely this lack of fixed referent, says Ahmed, that propels emotions to circulate between the two signifiers of "foreigner" and "insecurity." What makes them circulate in the first place is the force of association, which in turn, increases as each flow of circulation further accumulates into the historicity of norms that started to shape others as fearsome in the first place.[6] Consequently, those whose bodies were signified as "foreigner" by the administration *became* fearsome, thereby finding themselves confined within the discursive frame of suspicion and insecurity.

Looking at the revolutionary events through the lens of affective economies thus helps identify the sites where political emotions came to circulate and accumulate, thereby gaining in performative power. While the year 1793 saw revolutionaries develop an apparatus of control that was presented in the name of the Committee of General Safety and solely aimed at people of foreign origin (Wahnich 2010a, 44), it developed a sustained affective economy. Making foreigners the scapegoats for all insecurities of the time,[7]

the circulation of suspicion slid from a general understanding of foreignness
to a particular one, classifying them as potential traitors and building up the
nation-state's exclusionary boundaries. The more that emotions of suspicion
circulated, the stronger the mechanisms of exclusion became. As Wahnich
explains, "[when] facing the three figures of the foreigner—the isolated
man, the bad contra-revolutionary citizen, the stateless mercenary—the
guarantee enunciated by a trustworthy witness was no longer reliable. The
guarantee could not be of pure language, it had to consist of the prevention
of dangers: foreigners had to be watched and, finally, excluded" (95). The
means to watch and exclude were found in mandatory censuses and passport
controls, through which identities of foreigners—fluid and heterogeneous
as they were—became trapped in the classifying logic of administrative
practices (96). First, censuses were used to fix the domiciliation of people of
foreign origin to one specific locality, and gradually, to restrict their freedom
of movement in order to prevent potentially dangerous effects of foreigners
assembling (97). Second, foreigners' heterogeneous identities became primarily reduced to a passport, that is, a juridical document that defined them in
terms of names and territorial origin. To lack a passport came to represent the
incapacity to reveal one's identity. Such a lack of recognizable identity, then,
became a void in the classificatory mechanisms of administrative practices.
Judicially interpreted as a negative sign, the void triggered emotions of suspicion and called for immediate action in the name of general safety.

Territorial Foreigner: The Case of Mr. Scholler

I came to think further about the relation between such territorial administrative logic and affective economies as described by Ahmed when I found
the archival file of the Revolutionary Court's indictment of Mr. Jean Mathieu
Scholler, a man of foreign origin who was arrested on French territory and
deported on the basis of his foreignness. The record of the indictment is held
in the French National Archives in Paris, filed as one of the cases tried by the
court in 1793 (France 1793). It reads in part:

> The Court [illegible word] that there is no indication of any offence in the pieces
> [of evidence] at hand. However, as Jean Mathieu Scholler—who does not speak
> French and does not indicate either his means of subsistence nor the reason for
> his travel to France—can be suspected of espionage, [the Court] orders that
> Scholler be sent back to stand before the administrative authorities in order
> to [illegible] to be decided against him while gaining what is due to humanity
> and public safety, with an order to deport him outside of French territory in the
> shortest possible time.

What struck me was the absence of a concrete accusation in Scholler's trial. Instead, the sentence of deportation was grounded on the preemptive character of the security measures taken against him. Fully based on an economy of fear and suspicion, the court's reasoning emphasizes Ahmed's point that emotions are essential components in the construction of collective identities, and first and foremost displays the extent to which emotions circulate because they lack a fixed referent (2004a, 123).

Indeed, the central words of the court's argument read that "Scholler ... can be suspected of espionage." While the use of "can be" doubles the hypothetical meaning already present in the participle "suspected," feelings of suspicion clearly accumulate and mark Scholler's body as foreign *and* threatening. The absence of linguistic proficiency, financial means, and general information are the means for emotions of suspicion to do their work. Interpreted as a void, his unknown social, political, and financial positions become the kind of emptiness that slurps emotions while propelling them forward; in turn, such emptiness becomes the site where emotions circulate and accumulate, thereby gaining in performative power, justifying immediate action.

Doubtless, language was a subject of discord and contradiction during the revolutionary period. Although French language proficiency was one of the determining factors in the court's reasoning leading to identify Scholler as a dangerous foreigner, Rapport (2000, 17) notes that, knowing that a wide range of languages were spoken on French territory at that time, the "French language ... could not ... be one of the prime legal criteria for French nationality." Then again, Rapport's conclusion goes against the *Dictionnaire de l'Académie* [Dictionary of the Academe], which in 1694 defined the nation as "all the inhabitants of the same state, of the same country who live under the same laws and use the same language" (quoted in Rapport 2000, 17). What the Scholler case emphasizes, then, is that there is a substantial gap between the judicial, formal, and institutional realities and that of daily practices. Notwithstanding those multiple languages spoken on French territory in the eighteenth century, the Revolutionary Court sided with the formal Dictionary of the Academe, identifying the lack of French proficiency as a marker of foreignness.

Furthermore, as the court labeled Mr. Scholler as a danger to society (society referring both to humanity and to the public safety), it projected the defeating logic of the revolutionary claim to institute a universal juridical system. Labeling someone a foreigner according to territorial and administrative categories, yet referring to them as a social and political danger, the juridical discourse placed the notion of foreigner at the crossroads of political identity discourses and the bounded reality of juridical norms. In Wahnich's terms: "the word 'foreigner' [circulated] between a political discourse and a juridical discourse on identification" (2010a, 348). The Scholler case shows that, reflective of those dynamics observed in Ahmed's understanding of affective economies, such semantic circulation feeds on the premises of an affective economy of fear and suspicion according to which the notion of foreigner was associated with that of the traitor to universal values. It was in the name of public safety *and* in the name of humanity as a whole that Scholler had to be deported from French territory. What stands out is the performative effect of the accumulation of lacking. Not only did Scholler lack French proficiency, he also lacked financial means as well as being born in the nation. The superimposition of these shortcomings had a particular effect: it broadened the suspicious void at work in the judiciary, thereby pushing emotions of suspicion forward. Their circulation inscribed Scholler into the discursive space of foreignness *and* insecurity, marking his body as threatening and resulting in the court ordering his deportation from French territory.

Associated with perceptions of potential treason, the notion of foreigner thus came to be associated with that of foreign origin. In effect, the presence of foreigners revealed the administrative limits of the revolutionary universal project. In a vicious circle, their passport came to represent the limits of universality in the discursive juridical space of identification, thereby becoming the proof of the unworkable ideal of universal rights.

FROM UNIVERSAL TO NATIONAL
IN THE NAME OF SAFETY

Not only was the importance of territoriality in the definition of national identity revealed by the way people of foreign origin were assigned the status of foreigner. The constitutional act of 1793 also set clear limits to citizens' rights, as it states that "[the] exercise of citizens' rights is no longer valid after naturalization in a foreign country; after taking office or favors coming from a non-popular government; or after the condemnation to abominable or afflictive sentences until rehabilitated" (Amic and Mouttet 1812; Wahnich 2010a, 75). Confirming Arendt's statement that the potentially universal rights of the citizen were perverted into particular, national rights (1973, 231), such constitutional restrictions in citizenship rights stage the inherent correspondence between the notions of citizenship and national identity (Wahnich 2010a, 75). They first of all express the extent to which the nation-state declared to be one and indivisible (81), thereby demanding indivisible loyalty from its citizens. But they also point to the importance of the link between a territorial logic informing identification practices and the political epithet "foreigner," since territorial criteria are also pertinent to those recognized as citizens but who left French territory to live elsewhere. The conditions of the loss of citizenship and the conditions of one's eligibility for it stress one of the limits of the universal ideal of the Revolution: the impossibility of detaching the notions of national identity and that of citizenship from the category of territoriality.

While the conditions of the loss of citizenship will be further discussed in chapter 4, the Scholler case and its political juridical context show the extent to which the revolutionary modes of belonging and repression were supported by an affective economy that informed the categorizing logic of territoriality and the legal enforcement thereof. Security measures against people of foreign origin clearly stem from the paradoxical logic of the revolutionary ideals. Although the French state was supposed to incarnate a mythical figure that represented the interests of the universe as a whole, the interests of the community that was called "humanity" were in fact those of the French people (i.e., those of the *patrie*) (Wahnich 2010a, 29). In line with Arendt's analysis of the conquest of the state by the nation (1973, 230), security measures were taken in the name of the *patrie*'s interests (Wahnich 2010a, 30), not in the interest of the universal citizen. Consequently, the revolutionary hospitality—which had initially been enunciated for man as a human being—became a finite hospitality that could no longer be relevant for those whose sole origin turned them into suspects. In this sense, the revolutionary hospitality shifted from an ethics of hospitality toward a politics of hospitality.[8] While prescribing a conditional hospitality in the name of humanity as a whole, the revolutionary paradox of hospitality found ground within a discursive and administrative space linked to security matters. The law expelling foreigners was a means to appease a general anxiety, the latter circulating and accumulating through the presence of those labeled as foreigners, who bore the effect of the metonymic slide through which the term "threat" came to be applied to "the one of foreign origin."

First, the revolutionary discourse delivered its intrinsic contradiction by means of a juridical system that systematically unfastened the category of the universal as it generated a set of categories that defined the citizen in specific terms, while these terms were being defined by citizens themselves (chapter 1). Second, the importance of the territorial logic became central to the extent that the category of being born *in the nation* became superimposed on the category of being born *tout court*. This presents us with the question: Were these the limits of universality in the revolutionary discourse, or did the affective economy informing the territorial logic reach farther than the process of becoming a foreigner according to one's place of birth? The next chapter investigates the extent to which Olympe de Gouges's trial suggests that yet another condition was superimposed on the category of being born: the implicit demand of consenting love, relative to national legal and political structures.

NOTES

1. Although I use the term "discourse" in its singular form, it does not mean to suggest that there was but one kind of discourse during the Revolution. On the contrary, the Revolution was an event in which a great variety of discourses came to interact with or stand in opposition to one another as the public space was being redefined. This study is particularly interested in the discourse through which juridical norms were established and came to cooperate with a national logic. If these juridical-political norms represent a certain discourse that has obviously become dominant, it must nonetheless be noted that the so-called discourse is in itself a site of contestation, and results from a heterogeneous social ground whose lines of inclusion and exclusion were constantly shifting.

2. The English term "stateless" is an anachronism that does not do justice to Wahnich's original text, which reads "*sans patrie*," meaning not related to a particular country.

3. Retrospectively, such practices of classification strongly echo what Marieke de Goede has described in terms of politics of preemption. As she explains, "[the] politics of preemption addresses a situation in which there is the expectation of a radical or catastrophic threat that is nonetheless acknowledged to be uncertain and, to a degree, unknowable" (de Goede 2012, 49). The contemporary context of politics of preemption will be further developed in part III.

4. Once again, this law strikingly anticipates contemporary security measures linked to immigration policies. See for instance Mireille Rosello's analysis of the effects of the 1997 Pasqua law in France, which advocated the arrest of French citizens who offered hospitality to illegal migrants (Rosello 2001, 35–42).

5. Ahmed constructs her analysis around the case study of those speeches on asylum seekers given by the previous leader of the British Conservative Party, William Hague. Nicolas Sarkozy's speech on the theme of fighting insecurity analyzed in the introduction to this volume contains identical tropes.

6. For further discussion of the power of historicity in discourse see Judith Butler's notion of "performative iterations," according to which the historicity of norms form a constitutive power (Butler 1997).

7. I refer here to René Girard's (1986) interpretation of scapegoat mechanisms, according to which those being persecuted by scapegoat mechanisms are those whose crime is not so much in being different, but rather in lacking the difference that was expected of them. Following Girard's thesis, Wahnich (2010a, 99) acknowledges that the economy of suspicion leading the revolutionary principles of repression rests upon such scapegoat mechanisms. As she explains, "once designated and thus identified, the scapegoat appeases the mimetic violence and disengages the dissolution of the social tie, while potentially recasting it. What is at stake is the need to appease the public space and to recast a quietude concerning the designation of the frontier that separates members of the community and the worrying strangers. This frontier has become a necessity for the community not to have to live under the black sun of an overflowing suspicion. But this frontier cannot be merely symbolic; in order to be efficient, it needs to be spatially signified and to be accompanied by gestures

that designate the space of the frontier; it needs to concretely exclude by bringing foreigners back to the border of the city."

8. I borrow here Derrida's theory of hospitality, in which he expresses the double imperative bound to the double-sidedness of hospitality, which he describes as being caught between the unconditional law of hospitality (i.e., the ethics of hospitality) and the conditional laws of hospitality (i.e., the politics of hospitality) (Derrida and Dufourmantelle 2000). Rosello convincingly problematizes these notions in *Postcolonial Hospitality* (2001). If the context of her study is divergent from the objects addressed in this chapter, the content echoes problems linked to the revolutionary period. Where Rosello addresses the situation in which migrants face the politics of hospitality in a postcolonial Europe (and within France, in particular), I suggest that the French Revolution anticipated the postcolonial debate through its enunciation of universal human rights and its political project of emancipatory liberty.

Chapter 3

Becoming Foreign 2

The Nation and Its Affective Economies

> *L'amour de la patrie fait plus que des hommes, il fait des citoyens.*
>
> —M. de Cazalès (1790)

Chapter 2 has shown the extent to which the establishment of citizenship during the French Revolution relied on territorial norms. Although the concept of citizenship derived from a universal ideal, its institution proved to require a contained space, expressing normative and moral hierarchies tied to lines of belonging and repression. Consequently, the territorial norm influenced the definition of foreignness, whose meaning slid from a politically loaded connotation to a territorial one, resulting in the conflation of political foreigners with territorial ones. Significantly, this process of containment and exclusion was driven by the need to contain popular fears of treason. As a result, defining norms of belonging and repression on a practical basis went hand in hand with an affective dynamic; being associated with a discursive frame of suspicion and insecurity, those of territorial foreign origin became the target of a mechanism of control and repression.

This chapter goes deeper into the question of affect in relation to questions of belonging and repression within the establishment of citizenship centered on the case of Olympe de Gouges. Surely, de Gouges's place in the history of citizenship is a particular one: denied citizen rights as a woman in a time when citizenship was reserved for men, she was formally excluded from the category of citizenship but was nonetheless tried as a citizen who had put the revolutionary project at risk. Her case, then, enters a discursive space where the meaning of citizenship failed, while at the same time being negotiated and instituted. That she was denied citizenship, that she herself claimed citizen rights by mingling with the political quest of the Revolution, and that her death followed from her political act all invite consideration of her trial as an expression of the political struggles in and of the establishment of citizenship. In this sense, the analysis of her case helps come to grips with those mechanisms of belonging and repression governing political subjectivity. Moreover, her case forces us to look at citizenship from those perspectives that are commonly ignored because they do not clearly belong to it. But it is precisely this borderline that is of interest here: investigating citizenship from the perspective of its failure in order to call into question the very terms of its construction.

Accordingly, analyzing de Gouges's trial serves the purpose of understanding some of the precedents for current denaturalization practices, and to assess the technologies of government involved when people are labeled as a threat before being pushed out of the national community. This chapter focuses on the processes according to which the *Tribunal Révolutionnaire*, that is the Revolutionary Court of the Terror, came to identify de Gouges as a traitor to the *patrie* and as a political threat; it shows how her fate was informed by the court's mandate to contain popular moods of fear and argues that images of citizenship were not solely mobilized for emancipatory purposes but also contributed to making foreign those who were perceived as a threat. More specifically, the chapter exposes emotions and affect as seminal dimensions of those technologies of government instituting the categories of citizenship, foreignness, and terror.

OLYMPE DE GOUGES: A SUBVERSIVE AUTHOR

Olympe de Gouges was born in Montauban, part of the Languedoc region in the south of France. She is best remembered as the author of *The Declaration of the Rights of Woman* initially published in 1793 (de Gouges 2012). A counter-text to the Declaration of the Rights of Man and of the Citizen, initially published in 1789 by the revolutionaries, de Gouges's declaration "identified the legislator's exclusionary politics and attempted to include women and people of color in the founding charter of the French Republic" (Vanpée 1999, 53). But her literary legacy extends far beyond this single text: her passionate devotion to political ideals of freedom and equality are expressed in numerous theater plays, pamphlets, posters, and letters.[1] Each of them represents different aspects of her political engagement within a multi-faceted oeuvre, which reaches out to politicians as well as to the people in the street and which is characterized by its politically and formally subversive attitude. At a time when literature and politics were arenas reserved for men, de Gouges's willingness to engage so publicly flouted convention (Vanpée 1999, 47).

Jürgen Siess (2005) has shown the extent to which her writings make use of a specific literary address that systematically subverted the genre in which she wrote. Aware of the expected discursive forms in the genre of the open letter, for instance, she reappropriated them in order to open up a space of discussion in which she, as a woman, could give an account not only of herself but also of the condition of women in general (10–16). In 1791, she addressed an open letter to the queen, Marie Antionette, as a prelude to her *Declaration of the Rights of Woman.* In this letter, she systematically replaces the conventional term of address "Majesté" with "Madame," instituting a horizontal dialogic space between her and the queen in which she could speak woman to woman (14). Although the form of the letter does not disqualify her tribute of respect—the genre of the open letter being, by definition, a genre that institutes a certain distance between the writer and the addressee—de Gouges finds a way to subvert convention in order to reach out to her target audience.

Her willfulness explains in part the revolutionaries' understanding of de Gouges's writings as a disturbing voice that needed to be silenced. Although de Gouges cannot be described as a foreigner in the sense discussed in the previous chapter (she was born on French territory to French parents) her fate reveals that revolutionary republican narratives were able to construct her as a threatening other, making her foreign to the revolutionary project. Based on the Revolutionary Court's interpretation of her texts as being contra-revolutionary material, de Gouges was sentenced to death and executed on November 3, 1793. One of the main texts cited by the Revolutionary Court in its charges against her was her poster titled *Les Trois Urnes* (The Three Ballot Boxes) (de Gouges 1993b). A space of expression for the writer but most of all a space of interpretation for its readers, de Gouges's text gives cues to further understand the logic behind the Court's verdict.

DE GOUGES'S *LES TROIS URNES*: AN AFFECTIVE TEXT

De Gouges's poster *Les Trois Urnes* was meant to be hung along the streets of Paris. On this poster, de Gouges calls upon the people to speak up about the political situation. She denounces the tyrannical attitude of the revolutionary regime and demands an election to enable the people to choose the form of government they deem best suits them. She proposes that each citizen should be able to choose among the following three forms: 1) a republican government; 2) a federal government; or 3) a monarchic government (de Gouges 1993b, 247). Her claim was that these proposed democratic elections would restore the French revolutionary ideal to its true value:

In name of the endangered *patrie*, the President shall proclaim the free and individual choice for one of these three governments. ... Such means, which [are] as humanly decisive, shall appease the passions and destroy the parties. ... The rebels shall dissipate; the enemy Powers will be asking for peace; and the Universe, surprised and in admiration as it has long been attentive to France's disagreements, shall cry: *the French people are invincible*! (de Gouges 1993b, 248)

In terms of genres, de Gouges situates *Les Trois Urnes* among fiction, theatrical language, and realism. For instance, it introduces a fictive narrator in its title, which reads in full "The Three Ballot Boxes, or the Salvation of the *Patrie*, by an Aerial Traveler."[2] Furthermore, in all de Gouges's political writings, the tone of address is direct and to the point. But for those making use of a fictive narrator, the tone is more fiercely critical of the prominent leaders of the Revolution and the general revolutionary strand of social and political change. Following that logic, *Les Trois Urnes* opens within the fictional space of the narrator:

My name is *Toxicodindronn*; I come from the land of the mad people; I have just arrived from Monomotapa; I have covered the four parts of the World, more in dream than in reality; for our life is no more than a dream: Everywhere did I find the same men, mad and mean, duped and roguish; that is, everywhere did I find crimes and errors. But as extremes touch ends, and as the good always comes of the excess of evil, it seems that the essence of revolutions is to regenerate governments through the very excess of their perversions. French people, stop and read, I have many things to tell you. (243)

Characteristically, this opening deploys the theatrical language de Gouges made her own, for, as Janie Vanpée notes (1999, 56), "[i]f de Gouges's theatre was political, her political pamphlets were increasingly theatrical."[3] Theatrical techniques provided de Gouges with access to her target audience; despite her continuous efforts and ongoing textual production, she was still denied entry to the podium of the Assembly (to whom she addressed the majority of her text) (56). However this did not prevent her from reaching her goal. As Vanpée points out (1999, 57): "if she herself could not declaim her speech directly to her audience, she would have a third person [usually the current presiding secretary] play her role and recite her lines." In a similar vein, de Gouges's street posters functioned as a vital link between her and her audience. "Affixed to the walls of the city as posters, the pamphlets re-presented the scene of Olympe de Gouges addressing her interlocutors in front of the Assembly as a virtual street theatre for the broadest public possible" (57). Similarly, the aerial traveler in the opening scene of *Les Trois Urnes* enabled the text to reach out to the people in the street. As the narrator provides a theatrical voice to the text, it also makes use of a direct address to the reader ("French people, stop and read"), which adds to the theatrical and fictive description of its character.

Likewise, the fictional genre mixes with a realist and topical content, which here is the Revolution and its role in regenerating governments and fighting corruption. According to Vanpée (1999), such a combination of reality and fiction served a clear purpose; its assumed distance enables the author to act out her opinion and criticism on the Revolution by reappropriating the historical events to her own hands. Recalling the opening scene, the last two paragraphs of *Les Trois Urnes* explicitly comment on the combination of realism and fiction: "Indeed, citizens, it is a god who spoke to me for you; it is now the author who will speak by himself; think that I am an aerial spirit, a newcomer from the land of the madmen, which enables me to communicate with you" (de Gouges 1993b, 248). Although de Gouges's text explicitly used the aerial character as if it were a medium to transmit her message, it also hints at the actual author ("it is now the author who will speak by himself"), yet indefinitely postponing the moment in which de Gouges would reveal her name, as the last sentence of the pamphlet confirms: "I do not disclose my name yet; but if I can rescue my *patrie* from the abyss into which it is about to collapse, I shall reveal my name, and hurl myself into the abyss with her" (248). Here, the fictive narrator is clearly replaced by de Gouges as the author. The effect of such a combination of fiction and reality is theatrical in the first place, but it also influences the reading of the text insofar as it allows it to fluctuate between metaphorical spaces and explicit language, thereby investing the space between performative and descriptive language.

Such literary movement typically enhances the circulation of emotions, as it broadens the heterogeneous space of language according to which the meaning of words must necessarily remain plural. This is not to say, however, that only fiction has the ability to let emotions circulate. To the contrary, the coming sections argue that the law itself incorporates and depends on an affective economy that gives it both its legibility and its performative force.

THE AFFECTIVE FOREIGNER: OLYMPE DE GOUGES'S TRIAL

Even though de Gouges claimed that her texts' criticism of the dominant revolutionary discourse was intended to improve the revolutionary project, her trial shows that her texts were interpreted otherwise by the juridical body. Following her attempt to publish *Les Trois Urnes*, she was arrested and arraigned on charges of counterrevolutionary intentions, an accusation that, if she was convicted of the offence, meant being subject to the death penalty according to the law of March 29, 1793, which reads: "Anyone convicted of having composed or printed works or writings that induce the dissolution of the national representation, the restoration of the royalty or any other detrimental power to the sovereignty of the people, will be brought before the Revolutionary Tribunal and sentenced to death" (quoted in Blanc 1993, 32). It is tempting to see in this juridical article an enunciation of the revolutionary discourse caught in a discursive dynamic, which Wahnich has critically described as the circulation of increasingly radical discourses that agitate the transition to violence (2002, 891). The juridical discourse in force claimed to be the only possible definition of the Revolution. Its content precisely targeted other forms of discourse that would challenge the power relations in place. In this sense, the law facilitated a discursive hierarchy that not only gave the law power over life and death but also established a certain definition of the Revolution that could only be challenged at the cost of one's own life.

Nonetheless, Wahnich draws attention to another kind of economy, which, according to her, predominated in such revolutionary juridical texts. Leaving aside the analysis of the performative force of the narrated juridical discourses, Wahnich directs her interpretation of revolutionary events toward a study of the affective economy informing the Revolutionary Court (2002, 891). Based on archival parliamentary debates and reports, she gives voice to emotional narratives surrounding the making of the law. She concludes by stating that while legislators needed to respond to people's volatile and negative emotions, their function was to make legal discourse a means to control the circulation of those emotions. As she puts it (2002, 891), "the Revolutionaries had to be aware of the risks of violence and dislocation of society related to the rapid flow of emotions, while at the same time control-ling them precisely by the symbolic activity in which discourses participate— the discourse of the law in particular." Crucial here is the fact that Wahnich places the Revolutionary Court at the intersection of popular emotions and symbolic discourse, interpreting the court as that which guaranteed the essen-tial unity of the social structure (892). Standing in for the collective body, the Revolutionary Court provided it with an appeasing normative framework according to which individuals were categorized in terms of their emo-tional attachment to the symbolic language (892). It affirmed the distinction between social groups and constructed their respective identities: that of the sovereign people against those who denied its sovereignty or did not respect it (900–901).

Translated in normative, juridical terms, emotions of fear and suspicion became the fundamental justification of the Revolutionary Court. As Wahnich explains it (2002, 897), "the means to dissipate the fears of the people consisted in giving a new symbolic and normative form to the popular fervor.

As a result, one explicitly requested that the emotional sovereign power of the people be translated into juridical terms, in order not to become destructive." This means that paradoxically, the law became both a means to contain the violence instigated by the accumulation and circulation of emotions and a means to achieve the total exclusion—or even extermination—of those who were deemed not to belong to the collective emotional union. The prevention of one particular kind of violence both led to and legitimated another.

LOVE FOR THE *PATRIE*: A NORM OF BELONGING AND REPRESSION

It is striking that where the law both prevented and legitimized violence, its legitimacy was conditioned by an affective economy. The social need to contain the circulation and accumulation of emotions of love, fear, and suspicion made of the law a normative frame. The law's function was to channel collective fear and appease the collective body (Wahnich 2002, 896, 898). In that respect, Robespierre's speech to the parliamentary assembly on December 25, 1793 is revealing. As he declared, "The government needs to be extremely careful, for all the enemies of liberty are seeking to use the government's faults, as well as its most sensible measures, against itself. ... Who will draw the demarcation line between all opposite excesses? Love for the *patrie* and for the truth" (Amic and Mouttet 1812, 433), Robespierre acknowledged that the law alone was not enough to protect the government from its enemies. His proclamation reveals that an additional measure came to be implicitly superimposed on the universal potential of the law: that of the love for the *patrie* and for the truth.

It is beyond the scope of this chapter to review the philosophical discussion about the relation between love and truth in depth, but it is safe to say that Robespierre's statement exemplifies the normative effect of love when this emotion becomes ensnared in the political juridical discourse. Reminiscent of Ahmed's observation that the circulation and accumulation of emotions shape the surface of collective bodies (2004b, 2004a), the position of love in Robespierre's speech becomes a prescriptive criterion; it becomes a norm according to which the court may select the good from the bad citizen (by citizen I mean here all those who constituted the social body). Furthermore, Robespierre's criteria for distinguishing between the good and the bad citizen also reads as a case in point to clarify Arendt's conception of the "conquest of the state by the nation" (1973, 230). The principle of "love for the *patrie* and for the truth" is factually an expression of patriotic sentiments, giving the nation *patrie* a central place in processes of social cohesion, which Arendt assessed in the following terms: "Nationalism ... became the precious cement for binding together a centralized state and an atomized society, and it actually proved to be the only working, live connection between the individuals and the nation-state" (231). With Arendt's words in mind, we see that Roberspierre's prescriptive norms for defining citizenship's lines of belonging and repression clearly appear as an instance where the state structure was being perverted "into an instrument of the nation," and through which the citizen became understood in terms of a patriotic "member of the nation" (Arendt 1973, 231). His prescription of "love for the *patrie*" directly engages with Arendt's metaphor of "precious cement": love for the *patrie* and for the truth was indeed presented in terms of the cohesive device for society.

What Robespierre's speech leaves unanswered, however, is the question of how to recognize and interpret love in one's behavior or writings. If love for the *patrie* and for the truth established the boundaries between friends and foes of the Revolution, and thereby assisted the Revolutionary Court in classifying those worthy of citizenship and those worthy of persecution, then de Gouges's trial becomes a challenging case. The challenge is apparent, because, based on her writings, she would certainly qualify as a loving patriot. Her case therefore stages a decisive politics of interpretation and offers new material to ponder over the affective domain of the political juridical order. First, the court affirmed that "there is no possibility of mistaking the perfidious intentions of this criminal woman and her hidden motives, when one sees her, in all the works to which she at least lends her name, slandering and pouring large drafts of her gall onto the warmest friends of the people and its most intrepid defenders" (quoted in Blanc 1993, 27). On the other side, de Gouges wrote: "Each paper that fell into their hands was new evidence of my patriotism and my love for the greatest of all causes" (1993c, 259); "My detractors in vain provide a mean-spirited interpretation of the work that attracts me such cruel persecutions. It is the nature of this work that confuses them" (1993d, 249). While de Gouges protested that her trial was based on a false reading of her intentions, the court was convinced of the accusation against her. Based on the law of March 29, 1793, it sentenced her to death for attempting to challenge the established political order of the Republic.

Crucially, the court's judgment was not solely made on the basis of de Gouges's language. Beyond the reference to her text as a challenge to the republican parliament, the excerpt of the indictment shows that the negative interpretation of de Gouges's writings was caught in the circulating forces of an affective economy. Recalling Ahmed's theoretical point that "fear does not reside in a specific object," and that "it is the lack of residence that allows fear to slide across signs and between bodies" (2004a, 127), de Gouges's persecution reveals an expression of the affective grounds underlying the constitution of citizenship's boundaries. In fact, the lack of a specific referent is not only present in the identification of the lack of love for the *patrie* in the court's reading, but it also occurs in the court's arguments, if one closely reads the semantic field. For instance, the object of the court's claim is expressed in terms of de Gouges's "perfidious intentions" (*intentions perfides* in French) and "hidden motives." Now, while "intention" has a strong relative value (its definition depends on a contextual and subjective interpretation), the French word "*perfide*" means "that which is disastrous, dangerous, *behind* favorable appearances" (Larousse 2018). Hence, the court's conviction was factually based on something that was hidden behind a first appearance. In this sense, the court's holding conveys that the *appearance* of de Gouges's text did not necessarily look suspicious; it was rather what the court recognized as its underlying, hidden messages—as the use of the nominal phrase "hidden motives" further illustrates—that warranted the accusation of treason.[4]

The court's reliance on hidden motives clarifies the stakes of citizenship when bestowed through a political-juridical atmosphere of fear: an interpretive gap, where circulating emotions are stopped and acquire meaning. While emotions acquire semantic values, the affective economy involved shapes a differential framework according to which the sovereign people come to be positioned against the woman who was believed to have betrayed the Republic's interest. Ensnared in the circulation and accumulation of emotions, de Gouges's work procured an interpretation as fearsome and became the expression of emotions needing containment by the law of the Revolutionary Court. Being persecuted, de Gouges had to bear the effects of the symbolic discourse constituting her as foreign to the revolutionary event. In that respect, her trial becomes the expression of the difficulty to negotiate with emotions on a political and juridical level, and reveals a major paradox tied to processes of making and unmaking citizenship. On the one hand, love for the *patrie* was seen as the guarantee of one's agreement with the revolutionary political project, which was made clear by Robespierre in his December 25, 1793, speech to the *Assemblée*. Yet, prior to loving the *patrie*, one had to publicly agree to the political project or one was put at risk of being made foreign by means of persecution. For as de Gouges's fate made clear, even when it was formulated in terms of love for the *patrie*, political dissent was not accepted as an expression of love.

Caught in the affective economy of the dominant revolutionary discourse, her work was denied access to the realm of a citizen's rights while at the same time, it demonstrated their limits. After all, she was striving for the abolition of colonial and imperial power, she fully embraced the universal ideal of the revolutionary project, and her writings bear witness to her attempt to claim political subjectivity as a citizen. But her work was stopped in the circulation of emotions: new meanings were imposed on her words, she became the token of a threat, and the concept of citizenship failed to rescue her.

NORMS OF LOVE FOR THE NATION

Hence, embedded in the political struggles pertaining to the establishment of citizenship, de Gouges's trial is not only a source of fascinating empirical material but also sustains an overall theoretical point. As the analysis demonstrates, the labeling categories "socio-political threat" and "enmity" are not so much expressions of objective truths, but are instead the manifestation of an affective symbolic language that serves political purposes. De Gouges's love was not recognized as love but was instead reappropriated and transformed into fear in a gesture of repression. Informed by the juridical logic, the displacement of emotions thus contributed to the normative formation of a public enemy. As an institution, the law established a power relation according to which the beliefs and emotions of the people's representatives were those that informed the symbolic normative formation of exclusionary discourse. De Gouges's love for the republican ideal was fatally lost in the process of reappropriation and transformation.

In conclusion, while Wahnich's analysis is illuminating for exploring the role of emotions in the law, an affective analysis suggests that it might give too much credit to the need to repair what she calls a "popular injustice." As de Gouges's trial makes clear, de Gouges's speech acts both fed the economy of love of the revolutionary cause and the economy of fear that went against contra-revolutionaries. If the affective economy of the Revolutionary Court might well have supported a need to appease the popular violence by means of controlling it, it still resulted in an emotional, normative, and categorizing judicial organ that did not solely take revenge on those against Enlightenment ideals, avenging the larger population. Instead, it also exterminated those who, in an attempt to avoid the tyrannical effects of revolutionary events, dared speak out about the weaknesses of those ideals. It is then highly questionable whether the court really succeeded in appeasing the violence of the people. Instead, it installed a new sort of repressive violence, which primarily worked through the symbolic and controlling mechanisms of the judicial apparatus. In Arendt's terms (1973, 229–31), the court contributed to perverting the state into an instrument of the nation; it worked as an expression of the conquest of the state by the nation, with the affective economy at work being the driving forces of patriotic, nationalist narratives centered on *love for the patrie*. Indeed, love became "the precious cement for binding together a centralized state and an atomized society" (Arendt 1973, 231).

NOTES

1. Historian Olivier Blanc collected and edited all of her writings, which are now published in two chronological volumes under the title *Écrits Politiques* (de Gouges 1993a).

2. Such use of a fictive narrator (here present in the form of an aerial traveler) is a recurring feature in de Gouges's last political writings, which include *Pronostic sur Maximilien Robespierre, par un animal amphibien. Portrait exacte de cet animal* (1792) (*Prediction about Maximilien Robespierre, by an Amphibian Animal. Exact Portrait of this Animal*) and *Combat à mort des trois gouvernements, par un voyageur aérien* (1793) (*Battle to the Death of the Three Governments, by an Aerial Traveler*).

3. Next to theatrical language, de Gouges's writing also strikingly echoes Voltaire's genre of the philosophical tale, which, as Frederick M. Keener defines it, constantly brings to mind realities of thought, feeling, and motivation alongside unrealistic and even anti-realistic narrative elements (Keener 1983, 12).

4. In that respect, the court's reading becomes a paranoid reading, that is, a reading that pretends to be a triumphant advance toward truth and vindication, while it in fact performs a tautological theory of enmity tied to the notion of the inevitable (Sedgwick 1997).

Chapter 4

Becoming Foreign 3

The Nation and Its Juridical Community

Nié par le colonisateur, on actionne son système juridique

pour lui arracher des droits. Avocats et juristes deviennent

des hommes-clés qui investissent les espaces de décision politique

et installent, sans y prendre garde, les valeurs du vainqueur

qui les avaient formés … (il soupir). *…*

Chaque avancée libérait des germes dominateurs.

—Patrick Chamoiseau (2002)

Chapters 2 and 3 have focused on affective conditions through which emotions contribute to the institution of citizenship, also introducing struggles taking place within the juridical definitions of political subjectivity. While chapter 2 focused on the extent to which the term "foreigner" came to be associated with "the one of foreign origin," thereby placing the notion of territoriality as central, chapter 3 demonstrated the extent to which affective mechanisms of belonging and repression are entwined with juridical political practices of interpretation. We saw the extent to which love had become the ultimate demarcation line between citizenship-worthy and threatening individuals, yet leading to a paradox. A politics of love shaped the institution of citizenship; but citizenship—as an institution—shaped the definition of love. This chapter now aims to further explore the boundaries of the institution of citizenship, focusing on the dynamics of rights while examining the work done by the new juridical norms in defining the contours of France's political community.

The discussion about mechanisms of belonging and repression within the juridical institution of citizenship is context specific. Following the framework discussed in chapter 1, the context here is still a time when the citizen was installed as the central political juridical figure: it was the citizen who was meant to carry the universal ideal of the revolutionary project; it was the citizen who was meant to embody a new and emancipated form of political subjectivity. At the same time, the juridical landscape contained many a paradox. To start with, whereas the revolutionaries published their Declaration of the Rights of Man and of the Citizen in 1789, thereby proclaiming their universal ideal of freedom and equality, the *Code Noir* was still in use in the colonies. Initially established by Louis XIV in 1685, the *Code Noir* provided a legal framework for slavery, establishing protocols governing the lives and behaviors of the colonizers and the colonized, including the definition of what was legal and illegal slave trade (Sala-Molins 1987). Certainly debated by some of the revolutionaries (among others, Olympe de Gouges was a fervent opponent to slavery and colonization), the *Code Noir* was nonetheless kept alive and continued to justify the racial segregation within the French political juridical community until the abolition of slavery in 1848 (Sala-Molins 1987).

The nature of such paradoxes within the juridical landscape highlights the place of colonialism in this time of French history. Dominant and persistent, colonial norms have influenced questions of political subjectivity and its inscription in the juridical framework. It is then from a postcolonial perspective that this chapter addresses the question of rights and political subjectivity. Without doubt, the colonial difference yields material enough for another series of books. The aim of this chapter is not to discuss colonialism as such, but rather to introduce the colonial aspect implied in juridical norms of citizenship and nationality in order to make us aware of its fundamental role within the histories of technologies of government shaping citizenship. More specifically, the analysis pauses on mechanisms that have fostered or sustained, by means of juridical language, the definition of an Other as positioned against those recognized as citizens. Going back and forth between the time of the Revolution proper and its aftermath, the chapter explores a number of paradoxes, not for their polemical nature but instead to further understand the struggles at play in technologies governing citizenship. It introduces cases where the boundaries of the juridical political community were questioned, challenged, or revised, highlighting those mechanisms of belonging and repression at play in the juridical system. The first section discusses the dynamics of citizenship at the junction of politics and law, showing the extent to which the law operates as a governing technology. The second section focuses on the 1848 abolition of slavery decree, looking specifically at the decree's inclusion of deprivation of citizenship in its article 8. Finally, the third section presents and discusses the case of Mr. Furcy, who challenged norms of recognition in justice so as to gain his freedom as a man.

DYNAMICS OF CITIZENSHIP: BETWEEN
LAW AND POLITICS

As addressed in chapters 2 and 3, the territorial logic and the affective economy of the revolutionaries informed the accessibility of citizen rights, thereby denouncing the informal logic of the supposedly universal rights. But the right to possess citizens' rights was further complicated by an internal sanctioning mechanism, which, in some cases, would allow for the deprivation of citizenship after one had been awarded it. Such processes of deprivation were carefully analyzed by Anne Simonin (2008), who explored penalties of civic degradation from 1791 until 1958, drawing a connection between deprivation of citizenship and the notion of disgrace or unworthiness. Her main argument states that, while functioning as the hidden foundation of the revolutionary political morality, unworthiness became a seminal criterion informing political decisions about the deprivation of citizenship until the late 1950s. Caught in the penal code from 1791 onward, civic degradations made a moral code out of brotherhood, the latter functioning as an order of obligation (42). The notion of unworthiness then became a milestone in selecting the good from the bad citizens, which resulted in the original alliance unifying virtue with the law (16).

The inclusion of this notion of "unworthiness" in the law was concurrent with criminal law becoming the framework of the new public order, its primary objective being to defend the institutions and the new republican values (Simonin 2008, 39). Hence, criminal law's primary function was to safeguard the institutional structure believed capable of delivering a universalized society. As the citizen now defined the law while being defined by it, the demand was that individuals recognized as citizens entirely live up to the honorable values of the Revolution. Since the citizens were the institutions while the institutions were the citizens, there was no room to maneuver outside of the affects and effects of institutional values. This symbolic yet symbiotic equation logically implies that those who did not entirely comply with the institutionary code of conduct needed to be withdrawn from the equation. According to Simonin, it is at this point that criminal law intervenes: intrinsic to full citizenship, she explains, civic honor can only be withdrawn from the "bad citizen" by means of criminal law and thanks to the new penalty of civic degradation, which strikes by inflicting temporary indignity on the citizen who has dishonored himself (2008, 40).

First of all, being a citizen was understood as being a matter of honor, an honor that brought with it a set of civic and civil rights that enabled the citizen to actively participate in society. Second, criminal law was the governmental means to intervene in a citizen's behavioral space. Accordingly, citizenship was not understood as a contract between the government and the individual, but rather as one of the most fundamental bases of the societal and juridical system. Failing to act in accordance with the values of citizenship was thus interpreted as an act of betrayal against the country. Crucially, this means that revolutionaries did not consider the enactment of citizenship a private matter, but rather a public or even governmental act. Being a citizen meant being a representative of the state. Acting as a citizen thus meant acting on behalf of the government and its moral values. In other words, being a citizen meant acting as a subject of rights in the larger sense of the term, that is, acting as the one enjoying the rights granted to oneself *and* acting as the one representing the law in its institutional force. In Peter Sahlins's (2004, 215–24) terms, the citizen of the Revolution was not (or no longer) a legal subject, but a political one.

If the citizen was a political subject, then its definition had multiple meanings, and so did the term "foreigner." As Brubaker (1992, 47) noted in his study of citizenship and nationhood in France and Germany, "[as] a political epithet, … '*étranger*' could be used against nationals as well as legal foreigners." That the term "foreigner" was so volatile only confirms the blurring of the distinction between the political and the legal, which resulted in the welcoming of people from abroad to take part in the revolutionary process while a special police for foreigners was set up to specifically control newcomers. Confirming such epistemological struggle, Sahlins adds an important dimension to it, as he writes that "both key words [of the citizen and the foreigner] were largely unstable in their meanings; among their many uses, they formed the *rhetoric weaponry* of the National Convention deputies" (2004, 284). Acknowledging the presence of rhetoric in processes leading toward the recognition of political subjectivity has important consequences. It makes room for seeing the processes of making and unmaking citizenship grounded in more than mere technical argumentation. If making and unmaking citizenship is a rhetorical process, then we must remain alert to the arguments' emotional appeal (pathos), as well as to the ethical appeal (ethos) at play in the rhetorical act.

De Gouges's case, outlined in chapter 3, is a case in point for understanding how emotions are part of the rhetorical process central to the establishment of citizenship. The emotions present in her case created a relationship of difference and displacement: they linked actors to one another while positioning them in opposition to one another, leading de Gouges to a space of total exclusion. While the analysis in chapter 3 especially focused on the argumentative aspect of such affective economies, it is also worth pausing on the ethos involved. Referring to the ethical appeal, ethos points at the persuasive value of speakers or writers; it is about establishing a sense of soundness, moral character, and the will to do good toward others (Corbett and Connors 1999,

72). Accordingly, one's ethos reflects and speaks to the normative framework of the context from which one speaks. Its appeal—an appeal that positively connects the speaker to its audience—is based on the belief of a shared understanding of what is right and what is just. It speaks to the audience's intuitive understanding of those norms in order to gain consent, a process that eventually leads to the reinforcement of norms by means of their repetition.

Although ethos is usually addressed in reference to a single speaker or writer, we can also identify the ethos of a time, referring to the normative framework established by those involved in the institution of rights. In case of the French Revolution, we have seen in chapter 1 the extent to which norms were grounded in the ambivalent appreciation of citizenship, humanity and foreignness. We have seen in chapters 2 and 3 that norms of belonging and repression were set up based on a mandate to control popular emotions. What stands out is that drawing the line between citizenship-worthy and threatening individuals went hand in hand with the ambiguity of fundamental social, political, and juridical struggles. Far from being stable, social, political, and juridical norms were being challenged, questioned, and revised. Such societal struggles provoked an ethical appeal with many facets: it was right and just to appeal to universal ideals of freedom and equality, thereby doing justice to the revolutionary spirit of the time; but it was also right and just to guarantee the people's safety, which led to severing of control mechanisms, leading some to spaces of utter exclusion.

In short, as criteria of belonging and repression were being defined and negotiated, the struggles of the revolutionary times provoked a structural ambiguity within the political juridical system. Foucault's theory of modern power (1990, 2007a) explains in part the nature of such structural ambiguities. Focusing on those patterns of power that regulated the lives of political subjects, Foucault identifies a shift in forms of power that arguably took place around the Enlightenment. The shift occurred through the rise of governments substituted for sovereign power. A characteristic of sovereign power was, according to Foucault, the right to decide between life and death: although the sovereign did not enjoy absolute or unconditional power, in the case that the sovereign's power or existence was threatened, he would either require his subjects to take part in waging war, thereby exposing their lives, or punish them by putting them to death (Foucault 1990, 135–36). In opposition, Foucault sees a government as a new form of power that does not exercise a direct right over life and death but instead "exerts a positive influence on life, that endeavors to administer, optimize, and multiply it, subjecting it to precise controls and comprehensive regulations" (137). The object of power is still life,[1] but the mechanisms of power have changed: it is no longer only a matter of life and death, but instead a matter of normalizing what life means through technologies of government. As Foucault (138) puts it: "One might say that the ancient right to *take* life or *let* live was replaced by a power to *foster* life or *disallow* it to the point of death." Moreover, the power to foster or disallow life was developed within the domain of the law, where the law is no longer the sword wielded by the sovereign; instead, "the law operates more and more as the norm" across a variety of fields, ranging from medical to administrative matters (144).

The French Revolution operates right in the middle of such a shift of power, yet its dynamic also demonstrates that sovereign power does in fact not fully disappear from modern forms of power (Foucault 2007a, 106). Indeed, the case studies presented so far illustrate the paradigmatic shift pertaining to the establishment of the modern state, but they also contain elements that betray the remnants of sovereign power within technologies of government. For instance, the Scholler case discussed in chapter 2 revolved around the notion of territory, which Foucault identifies as a seminal feature of sovereign power (96). At the same time, the Scholler case also illustrates the extent to which that notion of territory participated in mechanisms of belonging and repression generated by a governmental will to maintain a level of public safety, which is more characteristic of governmental power (108). Likewise, de Gouges's case discussed in chapter 3 displays a practice of sovereign power over life and death, while at the same time showing the extent to which judicial practices were becoming a normalizing instrument in the definition of political subjectivity.

From the perspective of colonialism, the overlap of governmental technologies and sovereign power is even more flagrant. As David Scott (1995) argues, the political rationalities of colonial power entailed a transformation, "disabling old forms of life by systematically breaking down their conditions" and "constructing in their place new conditions so as to enable—indeed so as to *oblige*—new forms of life to come into being" (193). Surely, obliging new forms of life goes together with technologies of government using the law to normalize what life means through the definition of political subjectivity. At the junction of politics and law, the negotiation of citizenship and political subjectivity was at stake. Within those negotiations, the programmatic mission of reason that stemmed from the French Revolution and the Rights of Man (199) was confronted with the paradox of colonial forces refusing to grant the same rights and virtues to the colonial subject.

When we are thinking about the relationship between technologies of government and mechanisms of belonging and repression operating through the law, Rancière's reflections on the subject of the Rights of Man (2004) are useful. Next to pointing at the antithetical movement between man and citizen as embedded within the Declaration of the Rights of Man (as discussed in chapter 1), Rancière develops an understanding of the Declaration of the Rights of Man that is precisely at the junction of politics and law. His starting point is to identify two forms of existence of the Rights of Man (303). "First, there are written rights," says Rancière (303). "Second, the Rights of Man are the rights of those who make something of that inscription, who decide not only to 'use' their rights but also to build such and such a case for the verification of the power of the inscription" (304). In the first case, the Rights of Man are the "inscription of the community as free and equal" (303). Their existence as inscription makes of them a reality in itself; it provokes their ideal of freedom and equality to become visible in the first place (303–4). In the second case, it is the practice of those rights that stays central, coming with a power dynamic that challenges their ideal of freedom and equality; the Rights of Man then become the rights of those who have access to the institution of rights in the first place.

Crucial in Rancière's analysis is the tension between written rights and the access to rights. As Rancière stresses (2004), the point in the second form of existence of rights "is not only a matter of checking whether the reality confirms or denies the rights. The point is about what *confirmation* or *denial* means" (304). This suggests that the dynamics in place between the two forms of existence of rights might say a lot about mechanisms of belonging and repression constitutive of France's political juridical community. Questions that arise are: When someone sees their practice of rights revoked, what is being confirmed, and what is being denied? Inversely, when someone challenges the norms of repression, what kind of norms are then being revealed and revised? Such dynamics between the practice of rights and the establishment of norms of belonging and repression make up the core of the next two sections. The first section looks into the 1848 abolition of slavery decree, pausing on those norms prescribing the loss of citizenship in specific cases, while the second presents and discusses the case of Mr. Furcy, who fought in justice for nearly thirty years to gain his freedom as a man.

THE ABOLITION OF SLAVERY AND
THE LOSS OF CITIZENSHIP

In the winter of 1848, after a period that saw a temporary restoration of the monarchy in France, the revolutionary republican spirit recovered its political power, deposed the king anew, and reinstalled a provisional government. One of the most prominent republican politicians was Victor Schœlcher, undersecretary of state and the appointed president of the Commission on the Abolition of Slavery. Based on the commission's report, the governmental decree on the abolition of slavery was discussed and adopted on April 27, 1848. The decree, as well as the commission's report, was published in the official journal of the French Republic, the *Moniteur Universel*, on May 2 and 3, 1848 (France 1848). It reads in part:

> The provisional Government,
>   Considering that slavery is an assault on human dignity;
>   That by destroying the free arbiter of man, it does away with the natural principle of rights and duties;
>   That it is a blatant violation of the republican dogma: *Liberty, Equality, Fraternity*
>
>   ...
>   Decrees:
>   Art. 1. Slavery will be entirely abolished in all the colonies and French possessions.
>   ...
>   Art. 8. In the future, even on foreign territory, it is strictly prohibited for every French person to possess, buy or sell slaves, and to participate, either directly or indirectly, in any traffic or exploitation of that kind. All breaches of these directives will involve the loss of citizenship.

In relation to this chapter's exploration of the limits of the institution of citizenship, article 8 of the abolition decree is particularly interesting, as it explicitly mentions the potential loss of citizenship should one continue to engage in slavery or own slaves. In line with Simonin's thesis on civic degradation following an act of unworthy behavior, the sentence in article 8 of the decree expresses citizenship in terms of a political subject expected to fully represent the values of its public institution. Yet, in this case, the sentence also highlights a telling contrast between the punishments inflicted upon those who were still involved in slavery, and those inflicted upon slaves who disobeyed their masters. Indeed, while disobedient slaves faced the death penalty (Césaire 2004, 14), slave traders and slave owners were confronted neither with death nor with physical expulsion (as was the case with political dissent), but with the loss of citizenship.

Surely, as a staunch opponent of capital punishment, I cannot possibly suggest that the death penalty might have been a fairer sentence for those involved in slavery. But knowing that in France the death penalty persisted until 1981, questions must be raised about such unequal treatment. Was the outrageous weight of death as punishment not recognized as death or even murder? Or was the loss of citizenship considered to be an extremely severe punishment comparable to death? Last but not least, what does such discrepancy in treatment tell us about the force of citizenship?

Following Foucault's theory of modern power (1990, 2007a), the unequal treatment between slaves and citizens demonstrates the concomitant presence of sovereign power and technologies of government: slaves are being treated as the subject of sovereign power who holds the right over life and death; citizens fall under the regime of the law in its normalizing function. Yet the distinction between these two forms of power is further complicated if we follow Simonin's remarks that the loss of citizenship must be inscribed in the multiple ways of "dying" known during the revolutionary period (2008, 221). According to her, the diversity of ways of thinking about death under revolutionary law reveals the complex characteristic of the question of death under the revolutionary regime (221). Not that the Revolution was inherently lethal, but as the revolutionary law multiplied the ways of dying, it accumulated corpses, certainly, but mostly produced a peculiar kind of death, identified by Simonin as "the living-dead," at a scale unknown up to that time (221).[2]

Although the deprivation of citizenship can, as Simonin suggests, be understood as one of the multiple ways of dying during the Revolution, the crucial difference between physical and administrative "death" illustrates the power relations at play. In fact, death is not literally death for all. Instead, the concomitant logics of territoriality, affective economies, and juridical community led to a hierarchy of death penalties that illustrate the concomitant existence of both sovereign power and governmental power. In that respect, the loss of citizenship (i.e., civil and civic death) stands out as a means to avoid physical death for those who initially belonged to the juridical community (i.e., the community of those being born in the nation and conveniently loving the *patrie*) but did not behave according to the revolutionary universal values. In contrast, de Gouges's trial illustrates the extent to which the physical death of some could be justified in the name of humanity as a whole, humanity being paradoxically restricted to those who had control over the social, political, and juridical structure: French male citizens who adhered to the revolutionary cause and behaved according to the established code of conduct. Silently, yet effectively, such restrictive humanity also applied to the principles of the abolition of slavery. By reference to human dignity, to the republican dogma, and to the natural principle of rights and duties, the decree of the abolition of slavery fully reiterates the paradox of the universal rights of man. On the one hand, each man is born free and equal before the law. On the other, the law establishes categories of belonging and repression, carving out of the juridical system a space where some are decidedly freer than others.

Nonetheless, the physical death penalty and the civil loss of citizenship also have a common social denominator. In both cases, "death" appears to be associated with a notion of "ungrievable lives" (Butler 2009, 1–32), that is, with the outcome of what happens when norms operate to make certain subjects decidedly more difficult to recognize than others (6). Despite the universal ideal of the revolutionaries, the frame of recognition of the eighteenth century made slaves decidedly more difficult to recognize as full political subjects. Following Rancière's understanding of the subject of the Rights of

Man (2004), those defined as slaves by the colonizers had not yet full access to the second form of existence of rights. Instead, it was still white male political actors who put into action what *confirmation* or *denial* of rights came to mean. The abolition decree formally freed slaves from forced labor, but they were still caught in a social, political, and juridical infrastructure that was primarily beneficial to the white male bourgeoisie while it continued to de-civilize, brutalize, and degrade colonized people (Césaire 1972, 2).

On another level, the civil loss of one's citizenship produced social subjects who were deliberately made ungrievable by law. Based on the notion of unworthiness, the deprivation of citizenship was inscribed in the affective logic of the Revolution that ostracized those whose affection for the *patrie* did not or could not be recognized as consenting love. Consequently, the deprivation of citizenship constituted the penalty that reprimanded acts of *lèse-fraternité*, that is, the violation of mutual trust at the foundation of the social community (Simonin 2008, 51). The deprivation of citizenship hence gave meaning to the confirmation and denial of citizen rights; the deprivation of citizenship became part of those practices undertaken in the realm of what Rancière identifies as the rights' second form of existence, when rights move from mere inscription to being the "rights of those who make something of that inscription" (2004, 304).

Loss of Citizenship and Penal Logic

Given that the 1791 practices of deprivation of citizenship were included in the penal law, it is worth exploring a little further the legal position of the abolition decree. Is it still informed by a criminal juridical logic? If so, what are the principles that refer to this logic? And what does it tell us about the hidden foundations of the notion of denaturalization?

By framing slavery in terms of "an assault on human dignity" and "a blatant violation of the republican dogma," the decree's opening sentences reiterate the logic of the criminal law described in the first section of this chapter. Although the overall aim of the abolition decree is to abolish inhuman practices of servitude in the colonies, its primary aim seems to be to preserve the revolutionary republican values and their institution. That the abolition decree serves the establishment of republican values is confirmed by Schœlcher's declaration that "the quality of slave master becomes incompatible with the title of French citizen" (France 1848). His statement asserts that being a French citizen must be understood in terms of a moral behavior worthy of republican value. Hence, article 8 is stipulating the deprivation of citizenship in case the abolition decree's directives would be breached.

I suggest that such conflation of the notion of citizenship and the institutional values of the revolutionary project precisely led to the need to encompass various gradations of dying. For if citizens were in general understood as being inseparable from the government (i.e., citizens are the government and vice versa), it implies a certain impossibility to inflict the death penalty on them, since the lethal practices would directly affect the existence of the government. The primary effect of the deprivation of citizenship is then to performatively undo the equation between the citizen and the government, so as to enable the total subjectification of the individual to the political and juridical power.[3] Being deprived of his juridical personality, the individual was reduced to a state of marginal humanity.

While this section has highlighted those mechanisms of repression at work from within the practice of rights (the second form of existence of rights as understood by Rancière), the next section will explore a case where the norms of repression were being questioned, looking at the other side of the practice of rights. It delves into the case of Mr. Furcy, who combatted the norms of repressions applying to him by taking legal measures against the man who owned him as a slave. What we see in the Furcy case is the will of a political subject to claim the rights that he was entitled to according to their inscriptions, but that the administration in power structurally denied him.

FURCY'S STRUGGLE FOR FREEDOM: AN ACT OF CITIZENSHIP

I first came across the Furcy case in Mohammed Aïssaoui's semi-fictional tribute to Mr. Furcy's history (2011). Written in the genre of the novel, Aïssaoui's work primarily gives voice to a man whose full name has been lost in the history of slavery's silences.[4] The text is narrated in the first person singular, thereby giving the reader a generous access to the author's quest for Furcy's traces in history, and constituting a rich source of bibliographical entries to nonfictional documentation of Furcy's history.[5] Reading through this reconstruction of Furcy's claim to the right of freedom, the reader balances between citations of historical discourses reproduced from archival documents pertaining to the Furcy case and fictional expressions of social and judicial encounters, where characters come to life in their historical context. My analysis below is primarily based upon the transcript of the final stage of the Furcy case, held in December 1843 at the Royal Court of Justice in Paris following an appeal in cassation, and now available for reference at the *Bibliothèque nationale de France* (Cour Royale de Paris 1844).

Central to the case is Furcy's determination to claim his right to freedom, as expressed in his first note to the public prosecutor, dated 1817: "I am Furcy. I was born free in the Routier house, to the free Indian woman Madeleine, then in the service of this family. I have been held as a slave by

Monsieur Lory, son-in-law of Madame Routier. I claim my freedom. Here are my papers" (quoted in Peabody 2017; Gerbeau 1996, 353).[6]

Furcy was thirty-one when he addressed the public prosecutor. Following the death of his mother, he had found the paper proof that she had been declared a free woman by law, despite her condition of living as a slave until her death (Aïssaoui 2011; Cour Royale de Paris 1844, 1–2). Furcy thus seemed to have the written proof of his right to be a free man himself, freedom being in principle inherited by filiation (Cour Royale de Paris 1844, 2, 40–43). But it took him until December 23, 1843, to obtain the recognition of his rights (Gerbeau 1996, 353; Cour Royale de Paris 1844). Looking at his case, then, makes us dive into those political juridical struggles of the time; it gives us primary material to understand those processes according to which norms of belonging and repression were being challenged; it shows us what it takes for someone to exercise their right to claim rights in an exercise of citizenship and political subjectivity; finally, it propels us into the differential gap between the written existence of rights and the access to those rights, barred by the practice of those already having access to the institution of rights.

Colonial Configurations of Political Juridical Powers

The speech for Furcy's defense was held on December 9, 1843, by Maître Thureau, Furcy's lawyer. It opens with Furcy's details followed by his claim: his right to freedom. After having summarized Furcy's arguments, Maître Thureau proclaimed: "The reason why I'm standing here is to request the freedom of a man! I am invoking here, in his name, the most sacred principles of natural law, the most ancient and the most glorious maxims of our national law, the rules inscribed in our colonial legislation by means of religion and by means of humanity" (Cour Royale de Paris 1844, 2). Thureau's proclamation sets out seminal political juridical struggles of the time, showing at once the political juridical rationality of European Enlightenment caught in the context of colonialism. There is no doubt that the central claim in the message is about freedom; not freedom as a concept, but freedom in a particular form: freedom of a man. The first sentence accordingly refers back to the Enlightenment ideal of individual freedom as expressed in the first article of the Declaration of the Rights of Man and of the Citizen. While inserting freedom into a political juridical narrative, Thureau's second sentence then presents freedom in relation to a series of laws, from broad to specific: natural law, national law, and colonial legislation. Furcy's freedom, says Maître Thureau, would be inscribed in these juridical political narratives. In Rancière's terms (2004), Furcy's freedom is being invoked here in the first existence of rights: written rights.

What makes Furcy's case so complicated is the second existence of rights, that is, those power relations taking place within the political juridical institution of rights. If Furcy's freedom is inscribed in natural law, national law, and colonial legislation, then having access to it becomes contingent on the power relations involved in the practice of those laws and that legislation. Looking at Furcy's case, then, also forces us to look at the power dynamics at work in technologies of government.

The framework at hand here is thus the triangle of natural law, national law, and colonial legislation with Furcy's written right to freedom in the middle. In the excerpt above, each of the different areas of law is further characterized: natural law comes with "sacred principles"; national law is based upon "ancient and glorious maxims"; and colonial legislation is informed by "religion" and by "humanity." Far from being innocent, the characterizations of each juridical area reflect the political juridical ethos of the time. In line with the structural ambiguity characteristic of the time, freedom is inscribed within the vocabulary of emerging modern power expressed here by national law, colonial legislation, and the reference to humanity. While the term "humanity" refers back to the Enlightenment's universal ideal, the adjective "glorious" qualifying the area of national law gives away the centrality of the nation and its technologies of government in the political rationality at hand. At the same time, freedom is also inscribed within a religious and sovereign understanding of power, as expressed by the words "sacred," "ancient," and "religion."

Although still implicit in Thureau's opening declamation, reading the case further makes it clear that there is a caesura between the national law and colonial legislations, as we can read:

> Our *patrie*, gentlemen, has never wished to be defiled by the obnoxious spectacle of the man sold by man as a commodity. The prohibition of this dishonorable traffic has always been absolute, of public order, resulting, before the eighteenth century, from the general principle, and, since 1716 and 1738, from the formal text of the Ordinances. "The master of slaves will not be able to sell or exchange them in France, and will be forced to send them back to our colonies to be negotiated and employed according to the edict of the month of March 1738. (Art 11 of the 1716 Edict, and 13 of the ordin. of 1738)." (Cour Royale de Paris 1844, 35)

Here, the excerpt illustrates the caesura between the laws observed in France and those applicable to the colonized territories. It qualifies slave trade as hideous and unworthy of the metropolitan French customs, but at the same time notes that the slave trade was perfectly legal in the colonies. Such territorial differentiation illustrates the well-known racist approach of the colonial project. Although declared French territories in terms of properties and in relation to France's sovereign power, the colonies were nevertheless considered to be of such a different nature that metropolitan laws did not apply—except for exceptional circumstances (Grandmaison 2005, 49–50). Colonies were thus ruled by particular laws, inscribed in the colonial legislation, and enunciated by the French authorities. But the territorial particularity of the colonies was not absolute: although indigenous people were not granted any recognition in terms of political subjectivity or citizenship, colonial settlers benefited from the same rights as French citizens residing in the Metropole (50).

This distinction between national law and colonial legislation, including the power relations that derive from such distinction, contains in a nutshell the political rationality of the colonial project and its effect on the institution of citizenship. It further shows the concomitant logic of sovereign power and governmental power operating in a differential gesture: the colonial settler, citizen, was considered the subject of rights, enjoying direct access to the dynamics of power relations taking place within the political juridical institution of rights. On the contrary, colonial subjects faced colonial power in its centralized, sovereign form. They were barred from any direct access to the dynamics of rights, but became nonsubjects of rights when designated by the law in cases against them. In the *Code Noir*, article 30 expressed their incapacity to embody public functions, or to testify in civil or criminal matters (Sala-Molins 1987, 150). The latter denial of rights was soon slightly revised on pragmatic grounds since the population of people of color was at least ten times that of the colonial settlers'. Further normalizing the racist hierarchy, a slave was then allowed to testify in court but only when a white witness could not be found (151). In the same spirit, article 31 took away slaves' capacity to be claimants or defendants in judicial cases; they could only be represented in justice through their master (152). If articles 30 and 31 thus denied slaves any kind of recognition in terms of legal personhood, articles 32 to 39 still expressed slaves' penal responsibilities and fixed the penalties in cases of *delict* or *marronage* (154–69). Slaves were thus addressed by the judicial, but only to their detriment. Far from granting them political subjectivity in an act of recognition, the judicial functioned radically against them.[7]

Knowing the juridical political denial of subjectivity to those identified as slaves, Furcy's determination to claim his rights is even more remarkable. His fight, then, appears as an example of a man who claimed political subjectivity in the exercise of claiming rights. By claiming rights while being denied any official recognition, he constituted himself as a political subject capable of judging what was just and unjust. In Isin's terms (2012, 108–44), he "acted as a citizen," not in the strict definition of citizenship at the time, but precisely in the exercise of claiming rights. Following Rancière (2004), we see Furcy investing the space between the two existences of rights; he identified his written rights and put his life at risk to become part of those power relations taking place within the institution of rights. With regard to Foucault's theory of modern power (1990, 2007a), Furcy appears to challenge the sovereign form of power constituting him as a slave; he claimed the normalizing function of the law and demanded that its norm of freedom and equality be applicable to all forms of life—his included.

It took twenty-seven years for Furcy to obtain the official recognition of his right to freedom. The length of his fight illustrates what it takes to question and challenge those confirmations and denials inhabiting the space between the two forms of existence of rights. It shows the effective force of the law's normalizing force, practiced by those already having access to the second existence of rights, where the law is being practiced. Now, I cannot but be moved by Furcy reaching his goal, and I am also struck by the arguments held in court in defense of Furcy's freedom. Most of it revolved around the question of his mother being from India, and whether she could have been a slave in the first place. So a passage from the defense reads: "We must thus acknowledge that our colonial laws and the obnoxious prejudices on the grounds of which they are being justified only target the African race; and hence all other races are free, since no laws have forfeited their rights to freedom" (Cour Royale de Paris 1844, 12). The main argument here states that Furcy's mother, and hence Furcy, had been free people by law, since the colonial legislation did not target people of Indian origin. Such a claim is already worth attention for its racist premises, but what strikes me most is the French centrism expressed in the second sentence, which illustrates the tenacity of colonial thoughts and colonial norms still contained in the discourse of those arguing against them (the phrase "obnoxious prejudices" in the first part of the sentence makes it clear that Furcy's lawyer disqualified colonial legislation). Saying that all other races are free since no laws have forfeited their rights to freedom implies that laws would only exist from within the Empire. Freedom, then, becomes a condition dependent upon the Empire's juridical norms; the Empire is the one making laws—writing rights—and the one making something of that inscription, that is, verifying the power of that inscription. Those who are not addressed by the inscriptions of the law are nonetheless still understood as subjects; their own rules and customs are fully ignored, and the confirmation of their freedom remains contingent upon the dynamics of the Empire's legal narratives.

The operating juridical norms revealed, then, are the norms of a prevalent superiority of the dominant political juridical order governing French society. Indeed, just as exposed in the opening claim of Furcy's defense, freedom is framed *as a right*; it is framed by the language of the law, and its position is being assessed in relation to colonial legislation, national law, and natural law.

Yet the relationship between those areas of law bears the political rationality of the time. Reflecting the dynamics of power according to which some were recognized as worthy of citizenship while others where labeled as threatening individuals, the framing of freedom operating in Furcy's case confirms the presence of modern, governmental power where the law operates as a norm through a variety of discourses (Foucault 1990, 144). The notion of freedom within the Furcy case, then, appears as a condition of recognition within the realm of the law.

A preamble to institutionalized narratives of citizenship, Furcy's combat to claim his right to freedom highlights those mechanisms of belonging and repression operating at the limits of citizenship. What I find fascinating about his case are those dynamics that simultaneously enabled him to and disabled him from belonging to France's juridical community. Caught in the middle of the political juridical ambiguities of the time, Furcy's demand to become a free man by law directly speaks to the complexities of the juridical system when observed from its lines of belonging and repression. First positioned as a threat against the community of citizens, he nonetheless claimed his right to claim rights. By acting as a citizen while being repressed by the be same norms he was invoking, he unsettled the lines of belonging and repression, calling into question the law's normative principle.

THE BIRTH OF THE AFFECTIVE NATIONAL CITIZEN

By means of its quality to unsettle, contest, and revise the dominant jur-idical norm of recognition, the Furcy case aligns with the Scholler and de Gouges cases, where the limits of citizenship were equally being questioned, challenged, or revised. Read in juxtaposition to the abolition of slavery decree taking place in the context of the shift from sovereign power to modern power, Furcy's case highlights the nature of the relationship between the law and notions of political subjectivity. Within such a constellation, the law appears as the space where the notion of citizenship is contained, challenged, and practiced: the abolition of slavery decree embodies those dynamics of citizenship at the crossroads of politics and law. Furthermore, the decree expresses the differential understanding of political subjectivity in relation to citizens and the colonial subject; governmental power fosters the normative operation of its juridical definition; the Furcy case portrays Furcy as prac-ticing his "right to claim rights" (Isin 2012, 109), thereby both challenging and reaffirming the universal potential of citizenship in its juridical context.

Overall, the juridical narratives on rights and identity issued during the Revolution tell us that only those whose deeds or mobility did not cast a shadow on the reality of the universal ideal had immediate access to French citizenship. Whereas transnational mobility led to expulsion or even loss of citizenship, political dissent resulted in the death penalty. Those who, in one way or another, revealed the bounded nature of the universality of the Rights of Man were systematically removed from the territorial, political, and/or jur-idical parameters of the supposedly universal rights. By then, humanity was well and truly restricted to the categories informing the juridical narratives of France and its emerging national identity, confirming Arendt's understanding of the Revolution in terms of a conquest of the state by the nation (1973, 230). Where the categories informing juridical narratives superimposed a territorial logic combined with the demand for a consenting love for the *patrie*, Ahmed's presentation of "affective economies" (2004b, 2004a) comes and complements Arendt's understanding of the perversion of the state by the nation (1973, 229–31). Through the case studies of Scholler's and de Gouges's trials, Ahmed's and Arendt's theoretical juxtaposition expose affective economies as the driving force behind the conquest of the state by the nation. The Scholler and de Gouges cases make us observe (collective) emotions to circulate and accumulate, thereby shaping the surface of the col-lective body. Likewise, we see the collective body taking shape in terms of a nation-state, where the limits of the Rights of Man and of the Citizen are defined based on territorial *and* patriotic criteria, which the Furcy case further emphasizes.

The consequences are twofold. First is the revelation of one of the core paradoxes of the revolutionary ideal. On the one hand, love for the *patrie* was seen as the guarantee of one's agreement to the revolutionary political project—which was made clear by Robespierre in his December 25, 1793, speech to the *Assemblée*. Yet, prior to loving the *patrie*, one had to publicly agree to the political project. For as de Gouges's fate made clear, even when it was formulated in terms of love for the *patrie*, political dissent was not accepted as an expression of love. Caught in the affective economy of the revolutionary discourse, those feelings of love were instead appropriated by the dominant discourse and turned into feelings of fear and suspicion.

Second is the illustration of Isin's observation (2002, 5) that "the dom-inant groups have never been inclined to give an account of their dominance. Rather, [they] have always been inclined to naturalize their 'superiority' and the 'inferiority' of the dominated, interpreting the struggles that resulted in their domination as epic struggles against transitive and distant aliens and barbarians." The male, national republican dominance certainly resulted in their struggle against those of foreign origin and those unable to fully comply with the affective economies of the revolutionary discourse. Concretized in technologies of government that retrospectively gesture toward denatural-ization practices, those struggles led people of foreign origin to be deported from the national territory—and sent political dissidents to the guillotine.

While the dominant group naturalized their superiority through the vocabulary of the universal, they constructed juridical mechanisms of belonging and repression at the crossroads of territorial logic and affective economies. Accordingly, mechanisms of repression made themselves known through the set of conditions informing the classifying principle of judicial narratives.

Overall, the case studies around the French Revolution and its aftermath reveal that the various modes of estrangement from the upcoming national community are not mutually exclusive but belong instead to a concomitant logic of territoriality, affective attachment, and juridical norms of belonging and repression. They represent liminal cases where the notion of citizenship "failed" while pertaining to the production of a national juridical structure. It failed to retain the state structure's potential to act as the guardian of fundamental rights, regardless of one's nationality. It failed to recognize de Gouges as a patriotic, yet critical, citizen. It failed to embed Mr. Furcy, from the start, into its realm of recognition. From a genealogical point of view, those failures are determining events. They determine the formation of citizenship within the French nation-state and, as the coming chapters will show, resonate in future practices of denaturalization.

NOTES

1. Giorgio Agamben has written extensively on the extent to which life—bare life—remains the seminal feature of Western modern power (Agamben 1998). Referring to Foucault's thesis on modern forms of power, Agamben stresses the fact that modern power *includes*—although more concealed—the sovereign power over life and death. As he puts it (1998, 6): "Placing biological life at the center of its calculations, the modern State therefore does nothing other than bring to light the secret tie uniting power and bare life, thereby reaffirming the bond (derived from a tenacious correspondence between the modern and the archaic which one encounters in the most diverse spheres) between modern power and the most immemorial of the *arcana imperii*."

2. Simonin's interpretation of the loss of citizenship as death has been further echoed in recent political debates about the deprivation of citizenship in France. We can recall Danièle Hoffman-Rispal's vindication against a further broadening of article 25 of the civil code during the parliamentary debate of September 30, 2010, in which she called the deprivation of citizenship a "civil death penalty" (France 2010).

3. In cases of political treason by citizens, though, the death penalty did directly apply without a prior deprivation of citizenship (Simonin 2008, 236). This can be explained by considering an act of political treason as an act that inherently unfastens the equation of citizen and government.

4. I refer here to Gerbeau's thesis on the silence of slaves' history (2013).

5. While I was finishing this book, I was thrilled to discover Sue Peabody's newly published work (2017), which provides an academic biography of Furcy's life.

6. Translation by Sue Peabody (2017).

7. The article numbers refer to the first *Code Noir* of 1685; although the numbers changed, their content remained in the subsequent versions of the code until the abolition of slavery in 1848.

Part II

DENATURALIZATION IN TIMES OF WAR: MODELING THE SELF, CREATING THE OTHER

Chapter 5

From Belonging to Repression

Denaturalization and World War I

Reflecting upon the roots of denaturalization, Claire Zalc (2016) notes that since the French Revolution, the construction of French republican citizenship, followed by the definition of nationality, have gone hand in hand with concomitant processes of bordering and of exclusion. Chapters 1 to 4 have discussed a number of processes of bordering and exclusion pertaining to the construction of citizenship. The first one, territoriality, relates to the construction of the nation as a state, whereby territory, and hence one's geographical origin, becomes determinant in the appreciation of individuals in relation to the political community. The second, the demand for a consenting love for the *patrie*, marks an affective domain within the construction of citizenship: love for the *patrie* was seen as the guarantee of one's agreement to the revolutionary political project—which was made clear by Robespierre in his December 25, 1793, speech to the *Assemblée*. Yet, prior to loving the *patrie*, one had to publicly agree to the political project so that one's love would be recognized as such by governmental powers. The third, the juridical expression of France's political community, includes territoriality and affective boundaries but goes beyond that: it introduces those rhetorical dynamics at the junction between politics and law through which the definition of an Other becomes positioned against those recognized as citizens.

The chapters in part II further address such processes of bordering and exclusion pertaining to the construction of citizenship and nationality, now looking at denaturalization law as a technology of government in times of war. Divided between World Wars I and II, each chapter highlights how politics of denaturalization contributed to model a performative image of a national self. At the same time, politics of denaturalization helped define and create strangers across various registers: from spies during World War

I, to communists in the 1930s, to Jews and political dissidents during World War II.

This chapter starts with the first literal version of denaturalization law, which came to be inscribed as such within the French legal code on nationality during World War I, following a series of measures which, as soon as war was declared, were used to exert control over foreigners (Weil 2008, 60). The chapter evolves as it demonstrates how denaturalization came to represent the transformation of an exceptional measure into a normalized technology of government. Relying on parliamentary documents, including drafts by parliamentary and parliamentary correspondence from the decade following the war, the chapter establishes a map of those categories that had supported the normalization of denaturalization. It exposes an emphasis on the notion of national and public security, which was in turn embedded in an affective conception of national community.

THE INCLUSION OF DENATURALIZATION INTO THE CIVIL CODE ON NATIONALITY

The first law on denaturalization was passed on April 7, 1915 (Malnoury 1915). As Weil understands it (2008, 61), this first law "instituted—under the control of the State Council and then of the Supreme Court—a procedure for stripping French nationality from naturalized persons of enemy origin." From this first law, a distinction between new nationals and French-born nationals created denaturalization's faculty to institute a differentiated understanding of nationality. What were the lines of reasoning?

The most straightforward arguments from juridical experts, such as by lawyer Louis Malnoury in his commentaries on this first law (1915), stated that initially, denaturalization's differentiating principle between French-born nationals and new nationals was strictly conceived as a way to combat espionage during World War I. Denaturalization hence posed the principle of the possibility for the state, during the war, to denaturalize those French nationals who were former subjects of an enemy nation and who had retained their former nationality while acquiring French citizenship (14).

As Malnoury further explains (1915, 16–17), the clause on denaturalization came from a gap in the civil code on nationality. While the code was very strict on the acquisition of a second nationality (article 17 stipulated the loss of French nationality for those acquiring another nationality elsewhere) no provisions existed for those acquiring French nationality while retaining their former one(s). This posed a problem for legislators, as they saw a physical danger for France and its citizens in those new nationals who had remained subjects of enemy nations (predominantly Germans) (17). The fear for espionage was further exacerbated by the Delbrück law, a German law on nationality that went into effect on January 1, 1914, which authorized German citizens "'to acquire another nationality of pure show for the preservation of essential interests' ... while continuing to serve Germany, which 'remained their true homeland, by propaganda, espionage, voting, and if necessary the use of arms'" (Weil 2008, 61).

Those historical juridical interpretations clarify that in this context of World War I, nationality had become an indicator of friendships and aversions. It was loaded with affective values that had effect on various levels: it directly came to affect the lives of individuals, as they might gain or lose their nationality and be treated accordingly; but nationality also revealed itself as a juridical political tool that nation-states mobilized in order to respond to one another by means of legal norms. Because "[efforts] were made to protect the 'true French' ... and to protect the country from French nationals who might be enemy spies" (Weil 2008, 60), one's nationality(ies) became a marker of "truth" and allegiance. In Gérard Noiriel's vision (2007, 18), the use of nationality to such political ends was a consequence of the war of 1870. According to him, the defeat of the French army by Prussia, the territorial occupation that followed, and the humiliation caused by the Treaty of Frankfurt (which established France's loss of Alsace-Lorraine) put an abrupt end to the optimistic and progressive vision of the nation that had dominated before (19). It was no longer a matter of supporting the emergence of new nationalities, but rather a matter of defending one's own against others (19).

Nonetheless, the law of April 7, 1915, on denaturalization is explicit about the fact that its intended applications were restricted by clear contextual boundaries: the duration of World War I. Article 7 thus stipulated that "the present law will cease to be enforceable two years after peace is definitively signed" (quoted in Malnoury 1915, 60). Denaturalization's history shows, however, that it is decidedly easier to pass a law than to abrogate it; it shows the extent to which, once at work in the French civil code on nationality, the language of denaturalization began to perform. Denaturalization had become part of the vocabulary of nationality, gaining performativity as it gained historicity.

FROM SECURITIZING TO AFFECTIVE LANGUAGE

As I delved into the French National Archives containing official bills and parliamentary documents from the beginning of the twentieth century, including drafts by parliamentary members and parliamentary correspondence, it became clear that denaturalization's performative force was linked to a move presenting denaturalization as an evidently desirable and legitimate entry in French law. While reading those documents, I sought to establish a map of those categories that had supported the normalization of denaturalization. What I found was an emphasis on the notion of national and public security, which was in turn embedded in an affective conception of national community.

As was, for instance, a letter by the regional commissioner of the Alpes Maritimes (a southern region of France), dated March 31, 1921, and addressed to the minister of justice and civil affairs (France 1921).[1] In the letter, the commissioner voiced his opinion that denaturalization laws from the war era were not extensive enough because they only applied to new nationals who were also subjects of enemy nations. Based on one specific case, that of a naturalized citizen of Russian origin who was understood to threaten public security, the commissioner was of the opinion that denaturalization needed to be extended to "all naturalized French whose attitudes and machinations contain the quality to jeopardize the national security."

Similar lines of thought were expressed in a draft bill that aimed to amend the law of April 7, 1915 (France n.d.-b).[2] It is unclear whether the document concurs with the official version submitted to the Parliament; the document is undated and bears no official insignias except for the fact that it was written on Council Presidency letterhead stationery. Nevertheless, the explanatory memorandum's vocabulary and rhetoric are meaningful indicators of the juridical political categories that sustained the transformation of denaturalization. The narrative predominantly sheds new light on the juridical political perception of denaturalization: denaturalization no longer appeared as an exceptional measure of emergency in times of war; it was now envisioned as a normalizing aspect of the French civil code pertaining to nationality.

Central to the authors' argument was their vision of nationality as a "public contract" binding two parties—the state and an individual. In their view, such a contract should provide equal rights on both sides. If an individual can forfeit his or her nationality, the state should be able to strip someone of their nationality in order not to have an inferior status with regard to its new subjects. The authors were also of the opinion that if nationality serves an individual by granting him or her the benefits attached to it, then France would have the duty to grant French nationality only to those individuals arriving merely with the intention to serve the nation.

In both argumentative lines, a rhetorical personification of France is at work, which has a twofold and contradictory effect. It first feeds on the juridical language of contract, rights, and duties; as a nation, France functions as a legal persona. Yet this first equation is followed by a synecdoche, where "France" becomes the signifier of those ministers and civil servants regulating the French politics of nationality. Here, the equation between the nation and its subjects no longer holds. By definition, the national administration does not possess the same rights and duties as individual subjects of the nation.

The bill's explanatory memorandum goes on to mention that the law of April 7, 1915, had already granted the government the right, during World War I, to reverse naturalization decrees for those new nationals originating in an enemy nation. According to the authors, although the circumstances of the war had come to an end, "it remained nonetheless evident that, even in times of peace, the government would benefit from retaining such a possibility." Here, the verb "benefit" contributes to the lexical field of contractual relations aiming at services and benefits. But it also makes clear that denaturalization is not conceived of as benefiting both parties equally since the sentence explicitly attributes denaturalization's benefit to the government (as opposed to individual nationals).

From Exception to Ordinary Law: The Formal Establishment of a Differentiating Principle

Thus, clearly embedded within nonexceptional political ambitions, denaturalization's historicity appears to give parliamentarians the occasion to extend the term's performance beyond its original context. By staging denaturalization in the operationalizing field of "national security" and "public security," yet including its politics outside a context of war, the authors adopt a logic of urgency and exception that they displace onto the realm of ordinary law.

At first sight, such displacement resonates with Giorgio Agamben's theory of the camp as the *nomos* of the modern (1997, 1998). Indeed, denaturalization's transition from a measure in times of war to a measure of ordinary law endorses Agamben's theoretical point: "The state of exception thus ceases to be referred to an external and provisional state of factual danger and comes to be confused with juridical rule itself" (1997, 108). It is crucial, however, to remain cautious enough not to substitute the effects of denaturalization for Agamben's concepts of *homo sacer* and bare life. If denaturalization law may, to some extent, produce similar ambiguous orders as Agamben's notion of bare life, indicating a situation in which "[it] is literally not possible to say whether the one who has been banned is outside or inside the juridical order" (1998, 29), denaturalization politics is not so much about the inscription of pure biological life (*zoē*) in state's politics, but rather about establishing a symbolic—that is, discursive and performative—differentiating juridical political order.

The discursive mechanisms behind such a differentiating principle became prominently visible in an additional archival document: a note written by an anonymous head of an office, dated April 30, 1918 (France 1918). The note belonged to a file containing various parliamentary documents pertaining to bills on denaturalization law that aimed to amend those regulations at work during World War I. Merely entitled "*Note du directeur*" ["Note by the Head of Office"], the document must have been an unofficial draft, as it gives no mention of for which specific parliamentary cell the author worked. Yet, its content suggests that the author had taken part in the elaboration of the new bill pertaining to denaturalization; the argumentation in favor of new regulations on denaturalization is extensive and says much about the analytical link made between "national security" and the place given to new nationals in such matters. Its opening states that the law of 1915 (as well as its subsequent versions decreed during World War I) had not provided all the expected results when it came to public security. According to the author, despite the 1915 law that had enabled the review of all naturalization decrees enacted before 1913, there would still be too many "false French" citizens; those "false French," being unworthy of the title of "national citizen," would nonetheless, thanks to that same title, escape the safety measures executed against them: sequestration of their persons, of their goods, and expulsion.

What struck me in the document were the ways in which denaturalization is used to establish a link between security arguments and affective labels, subsequently affirming a differentiated vision of nationality according to which new nationals are not addressed in the same way as French-born nationals. While migration comes to connote insecurity, the head of office's rhetoric slides away from the contractual language of his colleague, adopting instead an affective vocabulary according to which sentiments become the core mechanisms of inclusion and exclusion. While (un)worthiness and (in)dignity function as criteria of inclusion or expulsion, the potential for treason (hence danger and insecurity) is solely identified with new nationals. As the note continues, the affective vocabulary is supplied by natural and health metaphors that reinforce exclusionary mechanisms at play. It reads in part:

> The public authority should have the possibility to repudiate the favor they had freely granted, and to root out from the national soil, for reasons of indignity, the foreigner who has not taken root and therefore constitutes an embarrassment and a peril. ... It is not in fact about judicially testing the value of a contract, the conditions under which it was drawn up, to play against an opposing litigant the complicated mechanism of presumptions and evidence. It is about cutting off a parasitic or unhealthy member from the national community.

A natural conception of national community emanates from the text. According to the text's metaphors, the national community would be soil with French-born nationals being naturally healthy native plants. Not paying attention to the fact that such a view of national community clashes with any republican conception thereof, the excerpt states that becoming a French national should mean taking root in such soil, implying a parasitic presence, should the process of rooting not take place. The notion of "indignity," however, blends the natural metaphoric language with a clear social and moral conception of national community. For "indignity" connotes persons, not plants nor diseases. We are thus left with a double performative discourse of exclusion targeting new nationals only—the ones susceptible to be parasitic and unhealthy for the national community, the ones susceptible to be treacherous and unworthy.

Although these texts are especially representative of the transitory period when denaturalization was transformed from an exceptional measure to an element of ordinary law, their dynamics resurface in the juridical debate that took place around the newly formulated law on national identity enacted in 1927. From then on, denaturalization belonged to the regular legislation on nationality. Still inheriting from the discourse on emergency that was created during World War I, the new legislation further emphasizes the extent to which nationality had become an affective, differentiating notion.

NATIONALITY: A MULTIFACETED WORD

Among the materials pertaining to the 1927 law on nationality, one of the documents that particularly caught my attention was the *Manual for Foreigners in France* written by the lawyers Lidji and Le Moal as an analytical clarification of the law (Lidji and Le Moal 1928b). In their study subtitled "Rights and Duties of Foreigners Before and After Naturalization," the authors identified a specific category of denaturalization that only applied to naturalized migrants ("naturalized foreigners" in their text). They justified it as follows:

> A foreigner who has acquired French nationality through naturalization is assimilated […] into a French citizen; but does this mean that this quality cannot be taken away if they prove not to be worthy of it? French-born individuals remain French even if they commit acts that do harm to their *patrie*; it is impossible, if we may say so, to "denationalize" them despite themselves. On the contrary, the foreigner who was granted French nationality by favor of the Government may […] lose the benefits of this favor. (105)

As the excerpt presents both the conditional aspect of naturalization practices and the unconditional quality of being born into a nationality, it retrospectively echoes both the exceptional law of 1915 and Sarkozy's 2010 Grenoble speech, stressing the need for a differentiated approach to nationality. First,

French-born nationals were considered to be French forever, while new nationals were still being referred to as "foreigners" in the text. Further, new nationals were French on the condition that they behaved according to the law.

To some involved in the debate, such lines of thought appeared problematic. For example, P. Louis-Lucas, professor in the law faculty of Dijon argued: "It is paradoxical to repress a certain attitude of hostility in the attitude of French nationals by acquisition, and to think that the same kind of repression doesn't apply to those who, being more deeply French, should be even more faithful" (quoted in Roman 1941, 77). But what is striking in Louis-Lucas's comment is his own argumentative paradox. While he remained suspicious of denaturalization because it installed a difference in treatment and expectation, he himself reiterated the divide between born nationals and new nationals. Indeed, by linking a higher degree of faithfulness to the acquirement of nationality by birth, his argument assumed a specific emotional relationship between the nation and French-born citizens.

Those two visions on denaturalization contain the core of the mechanisms according to which nationality functions as a pluralistic juridical notion. Despite Louis-Lucas's will to refute the exceptional regulation for new nationals, his argument further contributes to the discursive distinction that separates new nationals from born nationals: by thinking of faithfulness as being a pivotal element in the relation between the nation and the citizens, the argument alludes to a definition of national identity that is based on emotions.

This emotional component of national identity finds further emphasis in a scholarly legal study on denaturalization published in 1941 (Roman 1941). In his reply to Louis-Lucas's argument, Roman argues:

> Indeed, this differential treatment is not "paradoxical." It can be explained by the difference in nature between the two kinds of French nationals. Based on their origin, on their hereditary attachment, on their spiritual formation and on a long tradition, the first ones will draw steadfast sentiments that shall always prevent them from standing up against their motherland. Yesterday the others were still strangers. Most of the time, they grew up elsewhere; they have mores and customs that do not resemble ours. They will therefore be more easily inclined to behave unfaithfully towards their adoptive family. It is then fair to allow it to get rid of them. (77)

As the nation and nationality are entirely naturalized and sentimentalized, Roman's argument contributes to systematically opposing new nationals against born nationals. The narrative emphasizes the presence of affective tropes: expressions such as "hereditary attachment," "steadfast sentiments," "*patrie*," and "adoptive family" transform the notion of a national identity into a tri-dimensional image. Its point of focus is the relationship between the individual and the nation; the second dimensional axis develops into a juridical discourse, of which the law on national identity is the core structure; the third dimensional axis develops into an emotional understanding of national identity, of which the metaphor of motherhood is the core structure. However, because the discursive content of national identity remains located in the juridical discourse, the third, emotional dimension of national identity remains both restricted and hidden by the structures of law.

When nationality is understood in terms of a natural, innate identity, it becomes highly problematic to even conceive of granting it to newcomers, just as it becomes problematic to conceive of denaturalization for born nationals. This is further reflected in Lidji and Le Moal's text (1928b, 105), in which the denaturalization of a born national is expressed as a complete impossibility: "Individuals born French remain French even if they commit acts that harm their country; it is impossible, if we may say so, to 'denationalize' them despite themselves." The authors' use of the word "denationalize" instead of the expected "denaturalize" (the latter being used for the denaturalization of new nationals) further indicates the ambivalence of meaning inherent in the notion of nationality. First, it reflects the authors' embarrassment at even conceiving of denaturalization for born nationals, as the term denationalization does not directly convey the rupture of their natural attachment to the nation. But then, why use "denaturalization" for new nationals if their form of nationality is solely understood as an attribute and not a natural link? I suggest that, on the one hand, the chiasm in the use of denaturalization and denationalization reflects the superficial and deceptive assimilation of new nationals to born nationals; as such, the terms "naturalization" and "denaturalization" initially mask the structural difference made between born nationals and new nationals, for it conveys the possibility for new nationals to be included in the natural understanding of nationality. On the other hand, the use of the term "denationalization" in relation to French-born nationals—this taking place in a discursive context that particularly points to their naturalized and sentimentalized attachment to the nation—suggests that denationalization will not necessarily deprive them of their natural and emotional bond to the nation.

The sole concept of naturalization law further emphasizes the presence of variations in the understanding of nationality. For if naturalization is part of French nationality law, while nationality is at the same time understood as an innate, natural identity, then it becomes clear that nationality entails a caesura in the interpretation of its definition. On the one hand, nationality refers to familial and natural community, which allegedly generates a deep-seated and ontological link between individuals and the nation. This implies that one *is* French, that is, that one possesses an emotional identity as a French citizen.

On the other hand, nationality refers to an attributive quality. Granted to new nationals, nationality is in that case understood as an attribute, implying a mere semblance of attachment to the rest of the national community as one *has* the nationality. The radical difference between these two interpretations—that of being French and that of having the French nationality—logically allows us to conceive of denaturalization for new nationals only. Their nationality is being understood as an attribute that can be replaced or removed according to the circumstances.

Effects and Consequences

The double meaning of the notion of nationality sets up a power relation between born nationals (natives) and new nationals ("foreigners") according to which the politics of emotions prevails on the political and juridical structure of the nation. It dictates an argumentative line according to which foreigners and migrants will by definition be intrusive newcomers who may be welcomed under certain conditions but whose care and protection will not be granted by the *patrie*. In other words, they are allowed to come in the legal sense of the terms. They will be given the juridical instrument to be able to take part in society (i.e., the strictly formal feature of national identity), but they will not be regarded as the children of the *patrie*.

Such mechanisms of exclusive inclusion find further echoes in the way Roman (1941, 91–92) describes the effects of denaturalization:

> The naturalized [citizen] ceases to be French on the date that was fixed beforehand. He [*sic*] no longer has access to the advantages that the late quality [*qualité défunte*] would provide, and will have, for instance, to resign from his job, in case he was a public officer. ... The harm will be less if he acquires another nationality, which can be the nationality of his first origin. It will be a mere change in label, and the lost child will be reunited with a family to live at ease. Otherwise—and it may happen—he will mingle with the stateless people [literally: people without a *patrie*] and will share their uncertain condition, which is a serious inconvenience to which we shall return later.

The excerpt reveals the extent of the lack of emotional concern for those afflicted by denaturalization laws. Despite Roman referring to the effect of denaturalization as provoking the death of their acquired national identity ("a late quality" [*qualité défunte*]) (which raises the reader's expectation of a rather emotional discourse), the tone of the description of its consequences remains strikingly detached. Especially the phrase "it will be a mere change in label" contrasts with the systematic reference to the nation through the metaphor of the family. It suggests that the acquisition of a new nationality would be a trivial procedure. At the same time, it keeps referring to citizens in terms of children and to nations in terms of families, which raises serious questions about the triviality of the processes of naturalization and denaturalization. On the one side, the gravity of denaturalization seems to be acknowledged through the use of words such as "*défunte*" [deceased], "harm" and "lost child." But on the other side, the gravity of the situation is immediately dismissed through the use of formulations such as "it will be a mere change in label," "live at ease" and the frequent use of the verb "can" and of the future tense. While it does not show much consideration for where the denaturalized citizen should go, or even could go, it seems to assume that there are abundant choices for denaturalized people to get on with their lives.

However, it is known that in the 1920s, denaturalization meant expulsion from the country, or could even result in incarceration in a concentration camp should the denaturalized person be of an enemy nation in origin (Roman 1941, 69, 91; Malnoury 1915, 34). The lightheartedness with which Roman reviews the effects of denaturalization is misplaced and worrisome, as it shows that the double definition of national identity contains a dangerous element. Although it might just be the result of linguistic approximations and internal contradictions, it also allows the state to construct a narrative that justifies the expulsion of naturalized citizens. Not only does it justify it, it makes denaturalization a mere trifle. The lack of recognition for the possible emotional relationship between new nationals and their new country translates on a general level by disregarding the real emotional effects that denaturalization might have on them: the consequences of losing one's job, of having to leave their town and go somewhere else. In fact, it seems as though nobody really knows where they can go, and nobody cares where they would go. Because the focus is constantly redirected toward the metaphor of the family and its accompanying emotional tropes, those being excluded from the metaphor do not get any attention. Instead, they need to tackle the performative force of a legal discourse that constantly drags them back into the field of the suspect foreigner.

DENATURALIZATION: AN OTHERING DISCURSIVE PRACTICE

When we look at these early texts pertaining to denaturalization, two main trends stand out. The first one is the recurrent rhetorical arguments centered on security and emergency. Such rhetoric makes the language of denaturalization operate as an instrumental logic to maintain and secure the national community. In the context of World War I, denaturalization gave the state the possibility to take away someone's French nationality if that person was born in an enemy nation. Denaturalization was thus primarily meant as an exceptional law, during the war, to deal with spying activities. Article 7 of this first law explicitly stated that the law would cease to be enforceable two years after peace was definitively signed. What the history of denaturalization demonstrates, however, is that it is easier to promulgate a law than to abrogate it; it shows the extent to which, once at work in the French civil code on nationality, the language of denaturalization began to perform. Denaturalization had become part of the vocabulary of nationality, gaining performativity as it gained historicity.

The second trend that stands out is in the ways in which politics of denaturalization contributed to model a performative image of a national self. One of the alienating frames at work performs through the recurrent metaphor representing the nation as a family, with French-born nationals as the children of the *patrie*. Such logic of nativism both entertains a structural suspicion against (former) migrants and betrays a politics of nationality that structurally prioritizes those born as French nationals. Invoked in struggles of defining questions of nationhood, politics of denaturalization then contributes to label others as threats across various registers. For instance, this chapter has discussed how denaturalization was used against spies during World War I. The coming two chapters will now show that denaturalization also came to work against communists in the 1930s, as well as against Jews and political dissidents during World War II.

NOTES

1. Direct quotations are limited due to restrictions in reproduction rights.
2. Direct quotations are limited due to restrictions in reproduction rights.

Chapter 6

Denaturalization in the Context of World War II

Expanding Denaturalization before the War

There remains little known about denaturalization practices during, before, and the immediate aftermath of World War II in France or elsewhere.[1] Within the French context, the case that first drew my attention was Charles de Gaulle's *déchéance*, decreed on December 8, 1940 by the Vichy government and taking effect August 2, 1940. Considering his sustained devotion to France during the war, I would have thought that studying his case might say much about denaturalization. However, whereas I had expected to find a substantial amount of primary documentation (governmental notes motivating his denaturalization, news items on the topic, an appeal from de Gaulle or his allies, or even support letters from the people, for instance), I was soon to be disillusioned: the archival file concerning his case proved to contain nothing but one bare document indicating the date of the denaturalization decree. Any attempt to closely analyze the case would thus involve speculations about silences and gaps.

Still, de Gaulle's denaturalization is striking, if only because it remains largely unknown to most French people. I remember asking myself: What would it do to the French conception of national identity if French children were taught in school that de Gaulle had been denaturalized while leading the Free France resistance movement from London? And in retrospect, what does it do to us when realizing that a former President was stripped of his nationality while, at the same time, gaining such a position in the Resistance that, after the war, his presidency came as no surprise (Gough and Horne 1994, 2–3)?

These questions highlight the significance of remaining aware of knowledge politics; because knowledge is produced through the lives of concepts on one side and their politics on the other. In terms of nationality politics, the lack of discussion about denaturalization surely impacts on nationality's

performativity. It conceals the concept's omnipresent xenophobic and differentiating principle, thereby reinforcing a certain image of nationality
that needs to be revised. It is with such knowledge politics in mind that
I propose to address denaturalization practices in the context of World War
II. Before diving into a more systematic analysis, the chapter opens with
the close reading of a governmental note contextualizing denaturalization
practices. It then proceeds by focusing on the extent to which denaturalization was legitimized on the grounds of a rhetoric foregrounding security as
a central argument. The discussion revolves around a selection of parliamentary documents and ministerial notes, including the 1939 bill amending
the provisions pertaining to the forfeiture of French nationality, presented to
Parliament on December 22, 1939.

DENATURALIZATION AS "POLITICAL
WEAPON" AND *"JEU D'ÉCRITURES"*

While conducting fieldwork in the French National Archives, I discovered
box after box of documents related to denaturalization practices during the
war, ranging from ministerial notes, parliamentary documents, debates and
reports, bills, decrees and ministerial responses. A governmental note caught
my attention because its introductory paragraphs reviewed the scope of the
forfeiture of nationality thus far (France 1951b). The note was dated February
19, 1951, written in the name of the French Ministry of Public Health and
Population. It was addressed to the chair of the Commission for Justice and
Legislation in the National Assembly in response to a bill amending certain
provisions of the Nationality Code, including provisions pertaining to the forfeiture of nationality (France 1950). It reads in part:

> From 1940 to 1941, the "revision of naturalizations," which targeted those
> 500,000 people who had become French since 1927, transformed nationality
> into a *jeu d'écritures* [dummy entry]. ... At the same time, the forfeiture of
> nationality became a political weapon: besides the 125 cases of common law
> denaturalization, there were 375 cases of political denaturalization.

It first struck me that the figures of World War II no longer allow admitting
that denaturalization was an exceptional measure. But most of all, I would
argue, the note is important because it introduces a number of categories that
informed denaturalization practices at that time. They can be summarized as
follows: 1) the systematic revision of naturalization files, 2) the application of
standards derived from common law jurisdiction, and 3) political motivations.

Before going into an analysis of such issues, let me first stress what is at stake, starting with the following questions: What are the consequences of stating that only those latter 375 cases were *political* cases of denaturalization, as opposed to including those resulting from the revision of 500,000 naturalization files and those resulting from common law jurisdiction? In other words, is the systematic revision of naturalization files (a process that led to thousands of denaturalization cases, or millions, considering similar practices in other European countries at that time) not just as political, as the political disagreement that resulted in the 375 denaturalization cases (including that of de Gaulle)? On another level, is the interpretation of codified law not political in its own right too?

Additionally, the two expressions "*jeu d'écritures*" and "political weapon" encourage preliminary reflection. As "*jeu d'écritures*" is commonly translated into English as "dummy entry," the French expression further conveys that denaturalization practices are likely to be embedded in the heterogeneous space of language. In fact, literal translations of the phrase "*jeu d'écritures*" result in "game of writings," "game of scripts," or in "set of writings/scripts." Descriptively at least—but I suggest also performatively—the expression portrays denaturalization as the meeting point between heterogeneous language and rigid administrative patterns. The virtuosity of the legal scribe, who introduces some *jeu* as latitude in the system, is a vivid example of where law and language meet.

As for "political weapon," the phrase reveals the extent to which denaturalization is mobilized as a technology of government in a defensive battle: clearly, some territory has to be defended, and denaturalization is deployed as weaponry to this end. Moreover, the expression acknowledges the contingent character of denaturalization. Contingent in the sense that denaturalization belongs to a set of political norms and political beliefs that determine the ways in which one should act, think, and speak (that is, it establishes a set of moral and behavioral standards). Now, if denaturalization becomes a political weapon allowing a government to rid itself of those people expressing a fundamental critique while claiming a renewal of the body politic, then denaturalization is indeed a political weapon; a weapon that we would expect to be used by a totalitarian regime.

As this chapter addresses and questions those categories that have informed and legitimized denaturalization practices during World War II, I am particularly interested in answering the following questions: If denaturalization serves as a "political weapon" that participates in safeguarding the national community, which national community are we talking about? In other words, in the name of which community is authority being enacted when a denaturalization decree is declared? With those questions in mind, I plunged deeper into the stacks of archival documents.

LEGITIMIZING DENATURALIZATION: SECURITY RHETORIC AND NATIONAL COMMUNITY

December 22, 1939. The French *Assemblée nationale* was presented with a bill amending the provisions pertaining to the forfeiture of French nationality, submitted by M. Albert Lebrun, president of the French Republic, M. Édouard Daladier, minister of national defense, war and of foreign affairs, M. Georges Bonnet, minister of justice, M. Albert Sarraut, minister of home affairs, and M. Georges Mandel, minister of the colonies. Inscribed in the context of the upcoming war, the bill's explanatory memorandum drew on the law of March 19, 1939, designed to give the government special powers to take measures deemed necessary for the defense of the country (France 1939). This reference places denaturalization on two axes. First, the forfeiture of nationality was an exceptional measure that required special powers in order to be decreed. And second, denaturalization served as a measure to defend the country.

Although presented as a security measure, denaturalization did not, however, figure among the list of measures to take against individuals deemed to be a threat to the national defense and to public security (France 1941d). Does this mean that denaturalization was not a convincing enough measure to use against those deemed dangerous to public security and national defense? This is unlikely, as such a hypothesis contradicts all official statements on denaturalization; the notion of security is the most recurrent argument mobilized to legitimize denaturalization practices. Instead, I suggest that the 1939 bill rhetorically installed a security-related argument whose intended effect was not necessarily security as such, but rather the legitimization of denaturalization practices. In other words, security was invoked beyond its operational ground. The effect was clear: denaturalization became a technology of government employed in the maintenance of the national community. Relying on the idea that the nation had to be defended, denaturalization reciprocally mobilized and constructed a specific kind of national community.

The operational dynamic between denaturalization and the accompanying definition of a specific national community finds further emphasis in the explanatory memorandum attached to the 1939 bill pertaining to denaturalization, which reads in part:

> It might seem superfluous to provide a special law to amend the texts of common law. However, the state of war forces us to better adapt to the circumstances and to revise the modes of application pertaining to the principle of denaturalization.
>
> Indeed one cannot fail to recognize that during periods of hostilities, fraud by beneficiaries of acts of naturalization will be manifest with the greatest

evidence, and that the criterion of their sincere adherence to the French nationality will be most clearly established.

It has therefore appeared legitimate, during the period of hostilities, to extend the limits of denaturalization practices for denaturalizing foreigners who have acquired our nationality and, in addition, to extend the circumstances in which native-born nationals may be deprived of the French nationality.

The excerpt is telling for several reasons. First of all, it rhetorically installs a security-related argument as being central to the legitimization of denaturalization. Furthermore, it reveals the extent to which denaturalization relied on the ambivalent meaning of nationality. Finally, it provides insights into the flexibility and heterogeneity of the law.

In terms of rhetorical structure, the excerpt opens indirectly while employing a hypothetical (and therefore ambiguous) conditional mode: "it might seem superfluous …. however, war forces us to." Fostering the illusion that the reader's potential objections have been taken into account ("it is superfluous" being the supposed expression of the reader's objection), such an indirect opening functions as a form of address toward the reader, who nonetheless has no room to speak back. Instead, the form of address mobilizes a rhetorical pathos according to which the audience is expected to side with the authors, as the verb "to force" conveys that the forfeiture of nationality is the sole appropriate answer to the situation of war: "the state of war forces us to adapt better to the circumstances and to revise the modes of application pertaining to the principle of denaturalization." The effect is to silently shift toward the enunciation of a security-related argument that is posited as suitably central; an amendment of the law on denaturalization was required—and hence deemed appropriate—because of a state of insecurity.

The security argument is rhetorical in the first place, but it also gives away the extent to which the law remains susceptible to change, as it is inclined to be adaptable. Such flexibility and adaptability strikingly resonate with Foucault's understanding of apparatuses of security (Foucault 2007a). For Foucault, security is tightly connected to an operation of normalization that "consists in establishing an interplay between … different distributions of normality and in acting to bring the most unfavorable in line with the more favorable" (63). The term "interplay" reveals that security is a matter of action and reaction between various normative structures, a dynamic that affects a process of repetitive changes and adaptations. In Foucault's terms, "security … tries to work within reality, by getting the component of reality to work in relation to each other, thanks to and through a series of analyses and specific arrangements" (47). Furthermore, those analyses are grounded in the notions of risk, danger, and crisis (61). The norm is the result of a constantly renewed risk analysis, in which the expected behavior of the population becomes both a benchmark of normality and that which needs to be normalized and controlled. This means that while operations of security produce a norm according to which suspect behaviors can be differentiated from what is deemed "normal," the norm itself remains "an interplay of differential normalities" (63).

Emphasizing adaptability, on the one hand, and normalization processes, on the other, Foucault's approach to security is particularly helpful when scrutinizing the politics of denaturalization as presented in the 1939 bill. The bill states that denaturalization is a *principle* that not only works according to certain "*modes* of application," but that also has the capacity to be *adapted* whenever deemed necessary. In this sense, denaturalization can be compared to an empty signifier that facilitates and operationalizes normalization processes: available for semantic appropriation, it offers a structural space in which the constructed norm comes into operation.

But which norms are both referred to and produced by this normalization process? In other words, how does the bill pertaining to denaturalization feed on and produce normative divisions that affect the notion of national citizenship and, by extension, the notion of national community?

The Rise of New Limits to the Notion of National Identity

As affirmed by the 1939 bill amending the propositions pertaining to the forfeiture of nationality, the French national community is limited by the normative criterion of a "sincere adherence to the French nationality." Such formulation distinctively reproduces those mechanisms according to which processes of normalization remain by definition dynamic and adaptive. Generating a norm, following which the limits of the national community become operative, the text offers a criterion deemed suitable to identify those individuals who must be aligned against the national community. On the one side, national community is centered on the normative concept of national identity. On the other, national identity has no clear-cut boundaries; its limits depend on what is being done with it—the practice of denaturalization being one striking expression thereof. Hence the conceptual limits of national community being operative.

As denaturalization practices rely on subjective criteria, the boundaries of national community are drawn as a result of processes of subjective interpretation, which, in turn, depend on the flexible and adaptive capacity of the law. For what does it mean to sincerely adhere to French nationality? Who decides whether sincerity is sufficiently proven, and on which grounds? Clearly revolving around a word with a broad semantic content, "sincerity," the limitative criterion sets up a subjective norm that cannot be objectively defined. Instead, the manifest process of interpretation involved turns the normative criterion into interplays of differential normalities as it affects a process of repetitive changes and adaptation. Based on specific politics of reading and interpretation, the various approaches to nationhood invoked translate into operational concepts whose meanings evolve with and through the adaptive capacity of the law. As a result, practices of reading both instigate the law's flexibility and are at the core of those legislative (and judicial) processes through which specific normalities are being formed and defined.

One of the archival documents I consulted provided me with a vivid description of the politics of interpretation and adaptation. It came in the form of a typewritten note titled *"pour Monsieur le Secrétaire Général"* ["to Mr. Secretary-General"] and printed on stationery bearing the official letterhead of the Ministry of Justice (France n.d.-a).[2] Although not dated, the note may date from 1941, as it was clustered with other documents dated the same year. Its exact author and addressee remain unknown, the note being unsigned (which conveys that the document in question was a draft and not an official ministerial document). But its content reads as a response to a note by the minister of justice pertaining to the French politics of denaturalization, also evoking jurisprudence by the *Conseil d'État* on the matter. More specifically, the content begs the question of how to define the terms of "acts threatening the public order." This is one of the categories central to denaturalization practices: those who commit an act threatening the public order are liable to denaturalization. The note conveys that the minister of justice would have suggested it possible to define such a category objectively, while the author of the note, siding with the jurisprudence from the *Conseil d'État*, emphasizes the importance of keeping such a category subjective.

The first point in the author's argument is that the politics of a subjective definition is "both conform[ing] to the will of the legislator and reasonable." Regarding the first proposition (i.e., the proposition to conform to the will of the legislator), the argument denotes a strong normative principle in line with Foucault's understanding of security. Conforming to the will of the legislator, loose definitions such as "acts threatening the public order"—and by extension "a sincere adherence to the French nationality"—are "intentionally used" in order to "allow the government to pursue flexible policies so that decision makers will not be constrained in their work." In other words, such loose definitions allow regulation through adaptation.

However, where Foucault's approach to security emphasizes the population's behavior as a benchmark of normality, the note's argument proves to be primarily concerned with the space available for the government to act. The top-down practical logic of the argument is striking: subjective definitions clearly serve those in power to intentionally broaden their space of action beyond control.

The fact that such politics of normative adaptation are seen as reasonable tells us much about the discursive force of security rhetoric. Far from conceding that such a subjective definition extends the limits of the government's agency beyond democratic control, the note instead emphasizes that such politics of adaptation serve the "public interest." The argument reads as follows: "The same act can, at different times, constitute an act threatening public order."[3] In other words, acts that would not qualify as a threat at a given time might become threatening under new circumstances. This is why, according to the author, "it would even be dangerous to lock the jurisprudence into overly strict regulations." Indeed, the administration (be it the Ministry of Justice or the *Conseil d'État*) "must be able to maintain a certain freedom of judgment. The government must also have the ability to vary its politics of denaturalization by issuing more or less severe directives" [*"en lui donnant un orientation plus ou moins sévère"*]. As the author concludes, "[we] are in an area where the inflexible rules of law have been discarded by the legislator and must not reappear via an overly strict jurisprudence."

These arguments confirm the hypothesis that denaturalization finds legitimacy through rhetorical arguments centered on the notion of security. The starting point is to prioritize the interest of the national community. Besides, the note's concluding remark exposes the presence of a spatial temporal imaginary especially manifest in the word "directives" [*"orientation"* in French]. As interpretative freedom and adaptive politics rely on flexibility, they produce however directive forces with important consequences. They are the limits of inclusion to the national community; at the same time, they participate in the normalizing processes giving shape to the national community. "Oriented," such policies are the locus where practices of denaturalization operate a metonymic slide.

ENTANGLEMENTS OF LEGAL ADAPTABILITY AND PROCESSES OF NORMALIZATION

We have seen such metonymic slide at work during the French revolutionary period for instance, when a territorial logic started to label foreigners as suspicious, and when failing to prove one's love for the *patrie* meant finding oneself categorized as an enemy (e.g. Mr. Scholler's and Olympe de Gouges's case studies in chapters 2 and 3). In the context of World War II, one's governmental recognition as failing to be "a sincere adherent to the French nationality" led judicial and legislative bodies to associate these persons with threat and risk, which meant being aligned against the national community (1939 bill discussed above). Feeding on past associations (i.e., silently invoking the history of signs that is not necessarily visible or audible but that nevertheless participates in the performative effects of the sign at stake) (Ahmed 2004a, 120), the lack of sincerity created a relationship of difference and displacement. It offered an empty space that attracted emotions of suspicion requiring immediate action. Those persons deemed to lack sincerity needed to be expelled from the national community by means of denaturalization, which most of the time also lead to deportation.

Such metonymic slides, however, do not solely provoke movement. They also standardize as they become caught in administrative procedures. Despite the flexible quality of the concept of nationhood, a certain normative stability must be noted when it comes to defining the limits of the notion of national identity. Calling on past (and future) associations (see parts I and III), the 1939 bill (re)iterates the exclusionary equation between the terms of "new nationals" and "foreigners"; an exclusionary principle that finds further emphasis in the address to native-born nationals marked by the possessive in the phrase "*our* nationality." Considering the analysis pertaining to denaturalization during other time periods, the distinction between native-born nationals and new nationals acts indeed as a recurrent criterion. Its characteristic consequence is to privilege native-born nationals above new nationals in terms of an irrevocable right to national citizenship.

Stable as it might seem, this constant characteristic was nonetheless disturbed during World War II by the introduction of a new divide, now situated within the concept of the native-born national. For the 1939 bill deems it "legitimate ... to extend the circumstances in which native-born nationals may be deprived of the French nationality" (France 1939). Prior to 1939, native-born nationals could already be deprived of their French nationality, but in very strict circumstances: when they had acquired another nationality, when they had become a soldier in a foreign army, and from 1927 on, when they willfully served a foreign country as a civil servant (Malnoury 1915, 20–21; Lidji and Le Moal 1928a, 135–36). In short, the limitation of denaturalization on native-born nationals followed rules of territorial sovereignty, and prior to 1939, native-born nationals who had remained in France could not be denaturalized. Instead, denaturalization was aimed at new nationals deemed a threat to the national security. The thrust of the 1939 bill is to open up the scope of denaturalization: its primary target is no longer new nationals, but all nationals deemed susceptible to interfere with the national security. As a result, denaturalization started to work as a technology of government that reshaped the entire conception of national community.

Declared "legitimate," the bill's proposition institutes the premise—or even the promise—of a shared reference through law and becomes an expression of the complex relationship between law and the authority asserting the legality of the law. It thereby appeals to a certain notion of national community in which the content of the bill would find meaning and recognition. But now that some citizens (i.e., native-born nationals who were first affectively and even unconditionally included) face the risk of being excluded by denaturalization, whose notion of nationhood is being invoked? In other words, to which collective body (i.e., national community) and to which authority does the law appeal while seeking legitimization?

FROM *JEU D'ÉCRITURES* TO TECHNOLOGIES OF REPRESSION

The bill as presented to the *Assemblée nationale* on December 22, 1939, was not adopted before the installment of the Vichy regime. After consulting all of the *Assemblée nationale* proceedings for the end of 1939 and for 1940, I concluded that the bill had never been officially debated. There is in fact no trace of even a potential debate on any agenda. The spirit of the 1939 bill, however, resurfaces in laws dated July 22 and July 23, 1940, enacted by the Vichy regime: the law of July 22, 1940, announced that "one will proceed to review all acquisitions of French nationality pronounced since the enactment of the law on nationality of August 10, 1927" (France 1940a). One day later, the law of July 23, 1940 (France 1940b), decreed:

> All French persons who left the French metropolitan territory between May 10 and June 30, 1940 to go abroad, without a regular mission statement issued by the competent authority or without a legitimate reason, will be regarded as having sought to evade the loads and duties binding members of the national community and, consequently, having renounced their French nationality.

The latter law was amended by the law of February 28, 1941 (France 1941a), which stated that "the forfeiture of nationality will also be pronounced against all French people who, outside of the French metropolitan territory, betray by their deeds, speeches or writings, the duties binding them to the national community." A second amendment was enacted by the law of March 8, 1941 (France 1941b), in which it was decreed that the forfeiture of nationality would also apply to "all French citizens who, without authorization from the Government and as of December 1, 1940, went or will go to a dissident area."

Clearly, the national authority invoked in those texts does not refer to the national community in terms of all who consider themselves to be French. Instead, the national community appears as the sum of those being recognized as worth being French citizens by the government at that time. In fact, many of those who lost their French nationality as a result of the new directives never ceased to claim being French and to act on behalf of the French nation. The most salient example is that of Charles de Gaulle, who, based in London and leader of the resistance movement called Free France, never ceased to see his duty as being that of serving France, sustaining its autonomy and resiliency in the international context of the time (de Gaulle 1954). As François Bédarida's study (1994, 23) on de Gaulle and the Resistance confirms, "[de Gaulle] boldly proclaimed himself to be the leader, not of a foreign legion based in Great Britain, but of the French nation at war." Combined with de Gaulle's affective description of his patriotism in the opening of his memoirs (in which he explicitly refers to France as being *his* country, even describing its successes and errors as his own) (de Gaulle 1954), such a sense of duty toward France makes it unambiguously clear that the general never ceased to consider himself a member of the French political community.

Accordingly, the national community invoked in the bill is bound by the government's formal interpretation of the nation's limits. Performing both as a "political weapon" and as *jeu d'écritures*, the adaptability of denaturalization law reveals the power dynamics enshrined in legislative and juridical processes. As *jeu d'écritures*, denaturalization law makes use of discursive ambiguities to create new juridical political categories, thereby emphasizing the malleability of legal norms, and representing the ways in which language becomes a seminal factor that influences people's lives and realities. As a "political weapon," denaturalization law performs the consequences of such newly instituted boundaries. The security rhetoric involved ensnares the notions of nationality and citizenship into a frame of urgency, thereby stressing the affective load of its narrative. But the analysis shows that in practice, denaturalization law does not have security in mind. Instead, it operates as a technology of government that turns questions of inclusion and exclusion into matters of belonging and repression: notions of nationality and citizenship become vectors of a political enterprise to label subsets of citizens as a threat in order to expel them from the national community. As a technology of repression, then, denaturalization law confronts us with an authoritarian vision of a nation's structure in which those in power have—and use—their means to reshape the nation's exclusion circumference, which chapter 7 will develop further.

NOTES

1. Claire Zalc's recently published study of denaturalization practices under the Vichy regime (2016) comes as a rich and timely resource, just as Alix Landau-Brijatoff's visceral response to her discovery of denaturalization practices during World War II (2013).

2. Direct quotations are limited due to restrictions in reproduction rights.

3. This sentence was a handwritten addition to the manuscript.

Chapter 7

Denaturalization in the Context of World War II

France's Totalitarian Infection

Hannah Arendt's seminal book *The Origins of Totalitarianism* (1973) is a good place to return when questioning authoritarian practices in relation to the nation-state. First published in 1951, her work engages with the juridical political discourses of World War II, especially addressing the worrisome unpredictability of a political system whose adaptable juridical practices of interpretation prevented any form of genuine democratic control. She writes: "[Never] has our future been more unpredictable, never have we depended so much on political forces that cannot be trusted to follow the rules of common sense and self-interest—forces that look like sheer insanity, if judged by the standard of other centuries" (vii). More specifically, she draws attention to the role of denaturalization practices within totalitarian politics. As she tentatively formulates it, "one is almost tempted to measure the degree of totalitarian infection by the extent to which the concerned government use their sovereign right of denaturalization" (278).[1]

Aligned to the analysis of denaturalization proposed so far, Arendt's formulation of "totalitarian infection" produces an analysis of affective economies performing on the national community. While the term "infection" connotes otherness and parasitic takeover, it tellingly implicates the government—the latter being not commonly associated with otherness. In light of the affective economy at work in denaturalization practices, where flexible normative criteria have become a means to govern beyond democratic control, Arendt's formulation marks the tendency for governments to estrange themselves from democratic principles as they exercise denaturalization; infectious elements affect the national community in the sense that they infect its democratic health. When governments act to shape a national community only worth-while of the government's own normative framework, they dramatically reduce people's capacity to contest authoritative claims imposed from above.

In the French context, such estrangement from democratic control surfaces when the administration appropriates acts of political contestation to categorize dissent as proof of enmity. As previous chapters have shown, dissent is generally understood either in terms of "an act threatening the public order," an "un-sincere adherence to the French nationality," or the act of going abroad without the explicit consent of the concerned government. Adopting rhetorical arguments of emergency and security, the French government thus imposed its politics of denaturalization on those constituted as foes. Its behavior thereby perfectly ties in with Arendt's observation that "[denationalization] became a powerful weapon of totalitarian politics, and the constitutional inability of European nation-states to guarantee human rights to those who had lost nationally guaranteed rights, made it possible for the persecuting governments to impose their standard of values even upon their opponents" (1973, 269). The claim that the measure is appropriate because of the state of war (as claimed by the 1939 bill analyzed in chapter 6) does not stand up against Arendt's arguments. Anticipating any objections referring to a conceivable natural right to self-defense in times of hostilities, she indicates that "the behavior of these governments may appear today to be the natural consequence of civil war; but at the time mass denationalization were something entirely new and unforeseen. They presupposed a state structure which, if it was not yet fully totalitarian, at least would not tolerate any opposition and would rather lose its citizens than harbor people with different views" (278).

The French context of World War II offers a useful nuance to Arendt's perspective. Although it remains difficult to tell whether mass denaturalization was foreseen, there are at least signs that denaturalization was a controversial measure. This appears in the case of Thomas Olzanski, which sparked a significant protest (France 1932). Olzanski was born in Poland in 1886, a French citizen since 1922 and denaturalized on December 7, 1932, for having committed "acts contrary to the internal and external security of the French state" (France 1932). A militant syndicalist and communist miner, Olzanski had been labeled a threat to national safety based on his communist publications in *l'Enchaîné*, a biweekly publication from the North department (Weil 2008, 399). The archival file documenting his case testifies to the controversies it aroused among people and politicians alike. Often echoing the much wider political contest between the bourgeoisie and the proletariat, the file discloses numerous petitions calling the government to cancel Olzanski's denaturalization and expulsion. It also contains a number of protest letters addressed to the Ministry of Justice, as well as letters of advice from national and international human rights organizations warning the French government of the negative impact Olzanski's denaturalization would have on France's reputation. For instance, a protest letter from the *Comité Régonial*

Intersyndical Italien, dated August 7, 1932, notified the minister of justice that their trade union had "decided to make every possible effort to alert workers about the outrageous fact [of Olzanski's denaturalization], so as to denounce the so-called French democracy, whose methods are worthy rather of fascist countries." For some, at least, prewar denaturalization policies already looked dangerously totalitarian.

Furthermore, in France, denaturalization was not an entirely new measure. Its exclusionary logic had been developed since the beginning of World War I, and its structural insertion into the French civil code points at the French government's structural tendency to reserve themselves the right (in a literal sense) not to have to tolerate any opposition. Now, it may be too strong a statement to claim that France therefore never enacted its democratic principles but instead has kept functioning in a prescriptive and controlling manner.[2] But in terms of nationality politics, it must be argued that there is a credibility gap between the republican and liberal concept of nationhood claimed in all French official discourses and actual practices. Instead, practices of denaturalization betray a politics of national citizenship through which the nation's symbolic boundaries have been secured by means of a powerful exclusionary principle and based on a differentiated understanding of the concept of nationhood.

To such exclusionary ends, the adaptive quality of the law is crucial: it enables each new administrative political formation to redesign the limits of what is being perceived as acceptable opposition. Far from representing the necessary historical flexibility required to recontextualize ancient and sacred texts, the government's appropriation of adaptive practices betrays a crass authoritative logic, made unambiguous by the "Note to Mr. Secretary General" tentatively dated 1941 and discussed in chapter 6. The context of World War II further demonstrates the extent to which normative limits are flexible and the space available for contestation extremely narrow. While hundreds of French citizens were denaturalized because they had left the metropolitan territory without "a regular mission statement issued by the competent authority or without a legitimate motive" (law of July 23, 1940) (France 1940b), thousands of them were also denaturalized as a result of the massive and structural revision of all the naturalization decrees issued since 1927 (law of July 22, 1940) (France 1940a).

DENATURALIZATION AS SYSTEMATIC REVISION OF NATURALIZATION DECREES

The law of July 22, 1940, calling for the systematic revision of naturalization decrees issued since 1927 was a clear recessive response opposing the liberal politics of nationality as expressed in the law of August 10, 1927. It was then acknowledged that France faced a stationary population rate (due to a decrease in births and to the human losses caused by World War I), which was interpreted as a threat to the country as it lagged disproportionally behind European rivals such as Germany and Italy (Lambert 1928, 8). Besides, France was in need of a labor force (9–10). Conceived as a countermeasure to such socio-political challenges, the law of August 10, 1927, reduced the required time of residence in France for naturalization requests from ten to three years so as to ease and speed up the assimilation of foreigners into the French community (Lambert 1928, 8–10; Weil 2008, 68). As Weil notes (2008, 68), such a reduction went much further than the administration had ever thought and amounted to a departure from the traditional approach to naturalization. When with a ten-year requirement, "assimilation under the law confirmed a state of assimilation in fact," the shift to three years now substituted "prognoses" of assimilation for "diagnoses" (68).[3] The effect of the law was immediate: naturalization figures more than doubled in the first years following the law's introduction, reaching 22,500 decrees in 1928 and 1929 before stabilizing around an average of 17,000 in the following years (except for a peak in 1933 of 24,763 cases) (70).

Clearly, the law of July 22, 1940, pertaining to the revision of denaturalization decrees was a radical reconsideration of 1930s liberal nationality politics. It left an economic and trust-based logic behind (which had lasted only a few years) to make room for a politics in which those of foreign origin became again the target of sustained fears and suspicion.[4] But not every citizen of foreign origin was treated with as much suspicion. Although a significant number of European nationalities were targets of important denaturalization practices,[5] Jews were by and large the main victims of the 1940 revisionary measures (Weil 2008, 110).

"Of (No) National Interest": The Commission for the Review of Naturalizations' Working Method

The Commission for the Review of Naturalizations was not an isolated measure against Jews and people of foreign origin. On the contrary, it was part of a wide governmental gesture that did not only demonstrate an expanding anti-Jewish program but also developed increasingly severe restrictions imposed upon refugees (Marrus and Paxton 1995, xvii). As Marrus and Paxton consider it (54), "there was no sharp break in 1940; there was, rather, a long habituation through the decade of the 1930s to the idea of the foreigner—and especially the Jew—as the enemy of the State." Caught in an increasingly racial and xenophobic politics, in which economic, social, and political preferences were blatantly given to native-born citizens

(13–14), the work of the Commission for the Review of Naturalizations fostered a systematic recording of data concerning citizens of foreign origin. The commission also established bureaucratic links between information provided by the Department of Justice and Civil Affairs (under which the commission operated) and information obtained by police departments (Weil 2008, 110–11). Besides, it produced categories of denaturalization that distinguished between Jews and non-Jews (110).

The distinction between Jews and non-Jews reveals two contradictory forms of logic at work in the commission's working methods. As Weil writes (2008, 113), "Jews were denaturalized in the vast majority of cases—78 percent of the dossiers examined—unless they represented some 'national interest' for France or were prisoners of war. Non-Jews were denaturalized only exceptionally, if they had committed acts or expressed opinions that led them to be perceived as undesirable elements in the nation." What strikes me in such an asymmetrical logic of exception is the hollow quality of the criterion imposed on Jews: if being "of no national interest" leads to denaturalization, the content of the criterion cannot possibly mark a feared and threatening body to the nation.[6] Rather, as being "uninteresting" becomes reason enough for radical exclusion, expulsion and eventual extermination, the commission's working methods point to a specific affective economy where self-interest (enunciated in name of the nation) turns indistinctness into the material condition for difference and displacement.

It is against this background that Marshal Pétain declared that "[the] review of naturalization … [bears] witness to a firm will to apply … a unified effort at healing and rebuilding" (quoted in Marrus and Paxton 1995, 16). As noted by Marrus and Paxton (16–17), Pétain's formulation was typical of a general tendency to conscientiously avoid words like "anti-Semitism" or even "Jew." In effect, the "harsh fact of exclusion tended to be veiled behind formulas of a cautious generality" (17). For who would favor disease or chaos over healing and rebuilding (16)? Nonetheless, exclusion was clear enough, if only in Pétain's warning that "true fraternity is possible only within natural groups such as the family, the ancient town, the nation" (17). Unmistakably, exclusion was based upon a naturalized conception of what it means to belong to the national community.

The perverse outcome of the insidious, yet systematic registration of Jewishness was a well-understood fact for those resisting Vichy's collaborative regime. Voicing an anti-collaboration standpoint, public prosecutor General Mornet's note of December 15, 1941, (Mornet 1949, 120–21) offers the following reflection:[7]

Imbecility, foolishness, ignorance, natural reefs where despotisms sink. But there is something even worse than providing the enemy with jailers so as to keep the wretched tortured in Drancy; worse than sending police commissioners to arrest hostages in their homes: it is to identify—German killers only have to consult the *Officiel* or the official records of Jews kept in police stations. It is thus with a light heart that the government hands over the victims to the executioner.

According to Mornet, categorizing and registration practices were the most criminal of all, since they provided Nazi Germany with all the information required to arrest and deport those deemed inferior to the Aryan people.

As it seems to thoughtlessly participate in a bureaucratic machine of exclusion, the Commission for the Review of Naturalizations echoes Arendt's concept of the "banality of evil." Yet, was the commission as thoughtless as it first appears?

The Commission's (Banal) Evil

Arendt developed her thoughts on the "banality of evil" while reviewing the trial of Adolf Eichmann, an SS lieutenant-colonel who was tried by Israel in 1961 and sentenced to death for a series of ordinary crimes (such as the plunder of property linked with the murder of Jews) and for crimes against humanity (Arendt 2006, 244–47). By banality of evil, Arendt refers to "thoughtless" political obedience—and support—that SS officers and their bureaucracy owed to Hitler's politics leading to the Final Solution (xiv, 279, 287). She takes cues from Eichmann's statement that "he had never been a Jew-hater," that "he had never willed the murder of human beings," but rather that "his guilt came from his obedience, and obedience is praised as a virtue. His virtue had been abused by the Nazi leaders" (247). As a comment, she posits:

> The trouble with Eichmann was precisely that [he was] terribly and terrifyingly normal. From the viewpoint of our legal institutions and of our moral standards of judgment, this normality was much more terrifying than all the atrocities put together, for it implied ... that this new type of criminal, who is in actual fact *hostis generis humani* [enemy of all mankind], commits his crimes under circumstances that make it well-nigh impossible for him to know or to feel that he is doing wrong. (276)

In other words, the banality of evil finds its roots in the well-praised obedient attitude of bureaucratic staff, who, while following orders from above without ever questioning their content, do not necessarily realize the effect of their deeds (287). Moreover, the bureaucratic thoughtlessness of such methods of killing is based on a "principle of selection [which] is dependent upon circumstantial factors" (288).

In the case of the Commission for the Review of Naturalizations, the circumstantial factor was the law of July 22, 1940, promulgated by the Vichy regime and fully in line with the 1939 bill examined above. Composed and managed by the Vichy Ministry of Justice (article 2 of the July 22, 1940, law) (France 1940a), the commission certainly displayed signs of bureaucratic diligence as it boasted about the number of cases it managed to process in the first weeks of its activities (Weil 2008, 109–10). General Mornet voiced his critical view of the commission thus:

> It did not take me long to realize that the members of the commission were acting in perfectly good faith, trying to judge in full objectivity and in complete independence, and in most cases rejecting with distaste the idea of a policy of collaboration with Germany; but the majority of them, blinded by their trust in Pétain, made themselves auxiliaries of his racial policy and, even while denying that they were anti-Semitic, alongside decisions that were justified a hundred times over they nevertheless pronounced withdrawals of nationality that only a preconceived idea regarding Jews could explain. (quoted in Weil 2008, 118)

If Mornet is correct, then the commission did obey and support the Vichy regime thoughtlessly, applying the categories as stated in the law without even considering their moral or ethical foundations and consequences. In this respect, the commission could be seen as a perfect illustration of Arendt's concept of the banality of evil.

Yet, considering the operational criterion "of no national interest" adopted in the denaturalization procedures instigated by the commission (Weil 2008, 111; Zalc 2016), questions must be raised as to whether such a selective principle is indeed as banal as it seems. In fact, a criterion such as "of no national interest" betrays specific working methods that require a rather thoughtful mode of operation, as they rely on a criterion that does not speak for itself. Clearly, the line between having been of national interest or not is a contingent and subjective one, which is drawn by practices of reading and interpretation (Zalc 2016). Accordingly, the commission could not have merely applied an automated selective criterion.[8]

Besides revealing thoughtful working methods, the economic connotation attached to the criterion "of no national interest" strikingly resonates with Ahmed's work on the cultural politics of emotions, where she identifies the ways emotions participate in the surfacing of communities by "involving relationships of difference and displacement *without positive value*" (2004b, 45). In Ahmed's terms, this means that "emotions work as a form of capital: affect does not reside positively in the sign or commodity, but is produced as an effect of its circulation" (45). Furthermore, emotions are "not contained within the contours of the subject" (45), but "produce the very surfaces and boundaries that allow the individual and the social to be delineated as if they are objects" (10).

Such affective mechanisms are perfectly in line with the operational mode of the commission, the latter producing relationships of difference and displacement (both literally and figuratively) by means of practices of interpretation involving the circulation of signs. But how do we further qualify the emotion behind the criterion "of no national interest"? Is interest understood in financial terms, its opposite being a sense of collapse, or at least, a sense of regression that needs to be taken care of? Is interest an emotion comparable to fear, disgust, shame and love? Or does it betray the absence of emotion, the emotional state being then, perhaps, a state of total indifference? But if the opposite of interesting is indifference, why then proceed to denaturalization and deportation? Why not leave these people alone?

Potential answers to these questions came from an unexpected direction, while I was still in the process of digging through archival material. One of the files consulted concerned a bill pertaining to the revision of denaturalization law, submitted by M. Hugues, Medecin, and Bayet and dated 1951 (France 1951a). It contained the official document of the bill, as well as ministerial correspondence on the matter. A note from the Department of Public Health and Population, addressed to the chairman of the Committee on Justice and Legislation of the National Assembly on February 19, 1951, made a point of going against the bill's proposition to turn denaturalization into an obligatory sentence as opposed to a facultative one (France 1951b). That is, the application of the sentence would no longer depend on the appreciation of the judiciary (the accused *can* be denaturalized in case x and y), but would apply automatically in the case when the criteria of its enunciation were met (the accused *will be* denaturalized in case x and y). According to the Department of Public Health and Population, denaturalization needed to remain an optional sentence. Part of the argument was expressed in the following words: "Denaturalization must be of a spectacular nature, hence discretionary and exceptional, at the risk of otherwise stressing, as during the occupation, its relative uselessness" (France 1951b, 6).

What struck me was the emphasis on the desired utility of denaturalization, and the claim that its application had been useless during World War II. Although interest and utility are not the same, they share a common register of commodification and objectification. What does it mean to say that nearly five hundred thousand denaturalizations had been "useless"? An optimistic reading of the sentence would possibly translate the statement into a potential disavowal of denaturalization: that denaturalization had been useless because it did not contribute to a more desirable national community. This is wishful thinking, however, if only because the note does not make a plea against denaturalization as such. Instead, the relative uselessness seems to point at the failure of mass measures to result in an effective technology of government when it comes to delimiting the national community's exclusive circumference. Denaturalization must be exceptional in order to attract attention and therefore achieve an effective result; it is literally the exception that makes the norm. A massive process of exceptional measures would prevent the norm from operating accordingly.

As a result, the juxtaposition of those expressions of "no national interest" and "uselessness" betray a crass tendency for those engaging in the politics of nationality to lose complete sight of the human character of the population. From this perspective, the emotion behind the category "of no national interest" radically differs from emotions such as fear, disgust, shame, and love. The irony of the argument that new nationals are more likely to lack allegiance to the *patrie* could not be more salient. On the one hand, denaturalization is being justified in the name of an affective community where new nationals are treated with suspicion because one doubts their affective attachment to the *patrie*. On the other, those administrating the denaturalization decrees fail to show any empathy toward the population they govern. Such irony ties in with the paradoxical exclusionary measures implemented by the Commission for the Review of Naturalizations. Whereas the commission pretended some semblance of watchfulness by requiring individual assessment, they nonetheless remained centered on a criterion that turned its subjects into trivial and radically disposable beings. In line with Ahmed's theory, the absence of value—or the acknowledgment of its indistinctness—produced both the outline of the nation's circumference and the material condition for difference and displacement.

DÉGRADATION NATIONALE: ECHOES OF DENATURALIZATION PRACTICES?

The Vichy government's totalitarian infection did not go unnoticed by those resisting its regime. Indeed, the provisional government (formed in Algiers in June 1944 under de Gaulle's command) declared its task to be to reestablish French republican legality, including punishing those who had collaborated with Germany (Michel 1980, 108; Winter and Prost 2013, 180). It is in this context that on April 23, 1945, during the first hearing of his trial, Marshal Pétain was accused of totalitarian intentions (France 1945). Declaimed by public prosecutor General Mornet (whose oppositional views of the Vichy government were quoted earlier), the accusation act concluded by accusing Pétain of having committed "the crime of high treason against the State's interior safety" and of having maintained contacts with the enemy in order to ease his (i.e., Pétain's) initiatives in correlation with the enemy's own

(France 1945, 8). After twenty hearings—during which the political struggles of World War II in France were excavated, cited, and reiterated—Pétain was sentenced with *dégradation nationale*,[9] the confiscation of his property, and ultimately death (France 1945, 386).[10]

Labeled from the start as one of the biggest trials in history (France 1945, 1), Pétain's trial provides promising material for reflecting on broad concepts such as enmity, betrayal, nation, and patriotism, but also on the rhetoric adopted by both parties in such political trials, as well as on the affective economies at play in such judicial processes. It would take this book too far astray, however, to address the entire case here. Instead, I propose to limit my reading to one specific aspect that came up in Pétain's trial: the so-called sentence of *dégradation nationale*, which labeled a citizen as "national unworthy."

In effect, the sentence of *dégradation nationale* reveals moments of internal disruption and failure regarding the politics of nationality. Based on the genealogical approach that this book embraces, such a moment of failure tells us much about the contingency involved when some values of sovereignty become institutionalized, while simultaneously, others are suppressed. In other words, the punishment of *dégradation nationale* helps us grasp the kind of knowledge politics governing nationality during and after World War II. Furthermore, although the sentence as such does not equate to denaturalization (the *dégradation nationale* was for instance regulated by different laws than denaturalization, expressed in the penal code and not in the civil code), studying its logic alongside practices of denaturalization is illuminating for several reasons. First of all, it further reveals normalities and normative divisions governing the national community. Moreover, the history of the sentence's constitution proves to be closely connected to denaturalization politics. In fact, those who had defended its promulgation had based their arguments precisely on a refusal to further practice denaturalization.

Promulgated on August 26, 1944, by the provisional government, the sentence of *dégradation nationale* belonged to the Resistance's endeavor to restore republican legality on French territory and bring those who had been involved in the Vichy government to justice (Winter and Prost 2013, 196–97). The motives behind the sentence, however, contain a number of paradoxes. As Winter and Prost remark (2013, 180), the "day-to-day business of bringing collaborators to justice and providing compensation to their victims … was hardly compatible with the will to respect republican principles literally." I propose to explore those tensions based on two primary documents: 1) the provisional government's debate on national indignity that took place in Algiers on July 10, 1944, and 2) the ordinance's explanatory memorandum (France 1944a, 1944b).

The provisional government's discussion was centered on the presentation by the Committee on Legislation and State Reform [*Commission de legislation et de réforme de l'État*], whose introduction to the debate presented the sentence of *dégradation nationale* as a new penal sentence in French legislation. According to the committee, the legislative corpus available did not provide sufficient options to punish the full spectrum of acts of collaboration (France 1944a, 147). The punishment of the most blatant cases could be adequately administered by the dispositions contained in the penal code or in the code of military justice, those dispositions being aimed at the maintenance of contacts with the enemy and offences against the domestic or external security of the state (147). But not all acts of collaboration would fall under those categories (147). For as the committee's clerk M. Dumesnil de Gramont stated (148), "It is clear that, unless we torture texts and let them say that which has never been in their author's minds, there are a great number of collaborative acts that do not fit the offenses expressed in the laws in force on June 16, 1940."[11]

Implicitly, de Gramont comments here on the limits of the adaptability of laws that already exist. His standpoint reads that it is essential to respect the spirit of laws in order to avoid pure tyranny. At the same time, this limit of interpretability marks the beginning of another space of adaptation: the possibility to abrogate some laws and add new ones, thereby modifying the overall shape of the legal framework.

The *dégradation nationale* was hence presented as the adequate measure to take in order to punish minor acts of collaboration. Yet, as Simonin states (2008, 367), the promulgation of the sentence of *dégradation nationale* was not just a minor disposition but a fundamental law. In her view, the sentence of *dégradation nationale* and the corresponding incrimination of national indignity were the backbone of the reestablishment of republican legality in 1944 (367). Her view meets the introductory paragraph in the explanatory memorandum of the ordinance of August 26, 1944, where the sentence of *dégradation nationale* was presented as a measure aimed at "the problems which arose from the necessity *to purify* the *patrie*, at the wake of its liberation" (France 1944b, my emphasis).

Noble as the provisional government might have thought their act, this notion of purification betrays a substantial knot in the logic at work in the sentence of *dégradation nationale* and the corresponding notion of national indignity. While the provisional government condemned the totalitarian infection in the Vichy government, the solution they proposed betrays a tendency to think of the structure of national community along very similar lines. For does not the term "purification" painfully echo the insane biological idea behind the Aryan race? This is not to say that de Gaulle's politics was driven by the same ideology as Nazism. But it must be recognized that when it comes to the politics of nationality, the absurd logic of purity proves tenacious and maintains a persistent paradox.

On the one hand, the provisional government recognized the totalitarian quality of denaturalization and accordingly annulled all denaturalization decrees pronounced according to the laws of July 22 and July 23, 1940 (France 1943; Winter and Prost 2013, 189–90). On the other, they restored a politics of nationality that did not fully discard authoritarian principles: the *dégradation nationale* remained based on a specific moral conception of the national community, deemed superior to other views, and practiced from above. Simonin (2008) analyzes such progression of nationality politics by stating that in 1944, this new crime of *national* indignity accomplished the *nationalization* of the Republic; it sealed the Republic's identification to France, turning all alternative regimes to the republican regime in France not *illegitimate* but *illegal* (680–81, my emphasis).

When specifically focusing on the politics of nationality, a salient paradox surfaces. The provisional government wanted to reestablish the republican legality of freedom and equality, positioning themselves morally above the Vichy government's politics. At the same time, the politics of nationality they had restored reiterated some of the unequal principles that made it possible for the Vichy regime to move forward with mass denaturalizations.

A significant expression of this paradox is to be read in the provisional government's discussion on national indignity that took place in Algiers on July 10, 1944. René Cassin, chairman of the Committee on Legislation and State Reform, made a point of clarifying why the sentence of *dégradation nationale* did not go as far as to withdraw the convict's national identity. Adopting a morally superior tone, he explained:

> Other people would have liked to see us go further, and, for instance, see us impose on those disinherited persons the loss of French nationality and to impose banishment.
>
> This question has led to heavy discussions within the committee, and we insist on saying that it was after due deliberations that we excluded those two related sanctions. Why? Because totalitarian countries have abused denaturalization practices; because they projected thousands and thousands of miserable beings into the world, whom we call stateless persons.
>
> The problem of statelessness is difficult enough to solve now. France, country of liberty and equality, cannot afford, in turn, to expel beings who have the right to a *patrie*, even if they are disinherited.
>
> This is why we did not create one single new case of loss of the French nationality, without, however, touching on those cases provided for by the laws and decrees existing under the Republic. We did not want to exacerbate the problem of statelessness by creating beings without a nation.

In a second stage, we did not want to add banishment to the loss of civil rights. A certain number of convicts will find out by themselves the way to foreign countries, and will voluntarily exclude themselves from the national surface.

We had and still have in mind those verses by Victor Hugo in which he condemns exile. Without touching on those cases of banishment provided for by existing penal laws (rarely enforced under the Republic), we thought it unnecessary to expand the field of banishment. (France 1944a, 151)

I find this excerpt extraordinary, if only for the extreme paradoxes it contains. On the one hand, it presents the sentence of *dégradation nationale* as an alternative to denaturalization. Because denaturalization resulted in totalitarian politics, and because denaturalization provoked the colossal problem of statelessness, it would be irresponsible for France to further practice penal sentences in that direction. But on the other hand, the committee showed no concern whatsoever about maintaining the denaturalization laws that were promulgated before World War II. This means that denaturalization could still apply in the cases that we know about, that is, for new nationals found guilty of committing acts that undermined the domestic and external security of the French state; for new nationals found guilty of having served the cause of a foreign country by acting in ways that are incompatible with the quality of being a French citizen and that undermine the interests of France; and furthermore, for new nationals guilty of having evaded their patriotic military obligations (law of August 10, 1927).

This turns the sentence of *dégradation nationale* into a punishment with more consequences than Cassin was ready to admit. For the *dégradation nationale* does not solely mean the loss of civic, political, and certain civil rights for the disinherited. As Simonin remarks (2008, 461), in sum, national indignity appears to constitute the "act incompatible with the quality of being a French citizen and against the interests of France, accomplished in the interest of a foreign country," which became the criterion to denaturalize new nationals in 1927. This means that the sentence of *dégradation nationale* did indeed produce a number of cases of denaturalization. Simonin reports that thirty people lost their nationality after having been convicted of national indignity (461).

The figure is perhaps trivial compared to the mass denaturalization figures of World War II, and proportionally perhaps insignificant compared to the 46,645 sentences of *dégradation nationale* carried out between 1945 and 1951 (Simonin 2008, 461). And yet, it betrays the tenacity of the unequal principle of the French politics of nationality. Clearly, the provisional government failed in restoring a politics of nationality fully based on equality. They failed to recognize in denaturalization *principles* the basis of a differentiated understanding of nationality that impinges on the potential for an equal politics of nationality. If the abrogation of all denaturalization decrees pronounced during World War II was a measure that can only be welcomed, it should not mask the more subtle mechanisms that made these mass denaturalizations possible in the first place. By pursuing denaturalization cases in French law, the provisional government in fact reproduced the patterns of differentiation according to which native-born nationals enjoy an irrevocable right to nationality, whereas new nationals have only access to a conditional nationality identity and citizenship rights.

DENATURALIZATION AS POLITICS OF BELONGING AND REPRESSION

The context of World War II presents three strategies of government in which denaturalization played a prominent role: the extension of denaturalization practices in the prewar period (chapter 6), the systematic revision of naturalization decrees during the war (chapter 7), and the *dégradation nationale* in the postwar period (chapter 7). All three cases emphasize the adaptability of the law when governments aim to model the form of the national community. What stands out is the programmatic and normative force of the concept of nationality, which turns the very concept of nationality into a mobile yet limitative notion. The value of looking at practices of denaturalization in the context of World War II, then, is to engage with what happens when the adaptability of the law expands to such an extent that its contours drift onto illegitimate grounds. Embedded in and produced by rhetorical tropes centered on the notion of security, practices of denaturalization demonstrate a politics of nationality that performatively manipulates the concept of nationality from above. As a technology of government, denaturalization becomes the expression of a political and bureaucratic play in which those in power give direction to the adaptability of the law.

Furthermore, denaturalization practices during and around World War II highlight the extent to which French politics of nationality is concerned with a hierarchical national community yet to be realized. Imbedded in such politics, denaturalization becomes a means to achieve this future-oriented political project. Based on a specific vision of republican morality, those administrating the politics of nationality systematically claim to act in the name of what they believe to be the only political model worth legitimizing— or even worth legalizing. The government's belief in such moral superiority becomes the justification for exclusion and expulsion. Taking place on both administrative and physical levels (both often going together), exclusion manifests itself through denaturalization and *dégradation nationale*, deportation and death.

This means that as a fluid demarcation line, the category of "anti-national" behavior prescribing denaturalization becomes catastrophically problematic. While denaturalization practices reveal that individuals are turned into disposable beings, the politics of nationality betrays a troubling dehumanizing character. Following a future-oriented logic of interest and utility, nationality becomes the means; the future-oriented image of the nation becomes the end. This future temporality remains rather implicit in the context of World War II, but the politics of nationality as conducted in the 1980s and 1990s reveals it to be the dominant feature of counterterrorism measures, which I examine in part III.

NOTES

1. The tentative style of the sentence substantiates Arendt's realization that her observation is not a universal rule, as she adds in parentheses, "it would be quite interesting then to discover that Mussolini's Italy was rather reluctant to treat its refugees this way" (1973, 278).

2. It is a broadly sustained claim, however, to recognize that the Vichy regime was more authoritarian than democratic (Marrus and Paxton 1995; Weil 2008; Simonin 2008).

3. The terms between quotation marks are direct citations from the Ministry of Justice, Direction des Affaires Civiles et du Sceau in their "Commentaire de la loi du 10 Août 1927 sur la nationalité" (Paris, August 14, 1927) (Weil 2008, 295). Furthermore, easing naturalization procedures went hand in hand with the inclusion of an extra clause according to which new nationals could exceptionally be denaturalized by means of the judiciary in case of fraudulent acquisitions (Weil 2008, 68).

4. The law of July 22, 1940, was not the first of its kind. While describing the roots of Vichy anti-Semitism, Marrus and Paxton (1995) link the 1940 policies to the decree of November 12, 1938, concerning the status and supervision of foreigners, which modified the generous naturalization law of August 10, 1927, in the following terms: "French nationality could be stripped from those *already naturalized* in the event that they were judged 'unworthy of the title of French citizen'" (56). Furthermore, such a xenophobic tendency has proven to be a latent quality of the French concept of nationality, already perceptible during the French Revolution and despite the revolutionary endeavor to include people of foreign origin into the revolutionary project.

5. Former Italians, Poles, Spaniards, Russians, Romanians, Turks, Germans, Belgians, Greeks, Swiss, Hungarians, Czechoslovaks, Austrians, Portuguese, Yugoslavs, and a number of persons of unknown origin were denaturalized between

1940 and 1944, amounting to 15,154 cases, as reported by Bernard Laguerre (1988, 10).

6. The criterion "of no national interest" was not exclusive to the working method of the Commission for the Review of Naturalizations. The same logic was at play, albeit in reverse mode, in the law of June 2, 1941, concerning the status of Jews (and replacing the law of October 3, 1940), which not only determined who fell under the law's categorization of Jewishness (article 1), but also prohibited access to and the exercise of public functions (a list of which was provided by the law) to Jews (article 2). In its article 8, however, the law of June 2, 1941, released Jews from such propositions in the following two cases: 1) For those "who provided the French state with exceptional services"; 2) for those "whose families had settled in France for at least five years and provided the French state with exceptional services" (France 1941c).

7. Mornet is most known to the public for his role as principle public prosecutor in the trial against Pétain after the Liberation.

8. The view that the commission worked according to a thoughtful mode of operation is confirmed by Marrus and Paxton's (1995) account of Pétain's standpoint on the prescribed denaturalization practices: "[Pétain] accepted the principle of denaturalization and even agreed to hand over the newly created stateless persons to the Germans, but 'he could not accept indiscriminate activity.' Among the Jews in question were those 'who had served France well.' Therefore, 'for the sake of his own conscience he wanted to examine each case individually'" (326). Pétain's statement was made in the context of a political disagreement between Vichy France and Germany. Planning for large-scale deportations from France, the Germans wanted to proceed to denaturalize entire categories of Jews *en bloc* (324). Although such a plan found some support within the Vichy government (Laval was reported as having initially agreed without, however, taking concrete action [324]), both Laval and Pétain eventually objected to it, thereby drawing a line in their collaborative politics (328).

9. The term of *dégradation nationale* is hardly possible to translate, but comes close to "national dishonor" or "civic degradation."

10. Pétain was eventually spared the death penalty because of his age.

11. The date June 16, 1940, refers to the provisional government's standpoint that after this date, the French government (i.e., the Vichy government) became unconstitutional, as it was a *de facto* government, as opposed to a legal government (Simonin 2008, 364–65).

Part III

TERRORISM, NATIONALITY, AND CITIZENSHIP: FRANCE AND BEYOND

Chapter 8

Of the Link between the War against Terrorism and Denaturalization

One of the contemporary symptoms of the concept of insecurity is the notion of terrorism, which represents one of the major security policy concerns in France since the 1970s. It is not surprising, therefore, to find it appear in the legal text regulating denaturalization practices. Indeed, the 1996 version of article 25 of the civil code legislates denaturalization for new nationals found guilty of a crime or an offence that qualifies as an "act of terrorism."

It is this particular focus on the notion of terrorism and its link to denatur-alization practices that I explore in this chapter. By tracing the political and juridical trajectories according to which the notion of terrorism has been inscribed in the law, and in the law on denaturalization in particular, I discuss the extent to which "terrorism," as a juridical political concept that lacks def-inite semantic content, affects the intersection between national citizenship and security in such a way that citizenship becomes subordinated to security. More specifically, I argue that while the notion of terrorism both participates in the denial of citizen rights and in the separation of the citizenry from those seen as endangering society, its ambiguous semantic content allows those in power to constantly review the boundaries of their own categories. The chapter starts by first reviewing and assessing the political debate pertaining to the notion of terrorism's inclusion in the law on denaturalization, before examining the French juridical definition of terrorism as such. The results set the stage for discussing the affective economy bound to the concept of terrorism, as well as questioning the political effects of juridical definitions and judicial interpretations.

THE INSERTION OF "ACT OF TERRORISM"
IN ARTICLE 25 OF THE CIVIL CODE

The context in which article 25 of the civil code was amended was a parliamentary bill pertaining to the repression of terrorism, which was debated from November 1995 to June 1996. The main object of the bill was to update the French judicial code pertaining to the fight against terrorism, both on the level of repressive measures and on the level of procedural measures (Marsaud 1995, 6). It responded to a series of terrorist attacks that took place, especially between 1994 and 1996 (Masson 1996, 17–18). There was the hijacking of Air France flight 8969 from Algiers to Paris on December 24, 1994; a bomb exploded at the Saint Michel subway station on July 25, 1995, and another one on the RER train line B, exploding at the Port Royal station on December 3, 1996. The suspects were members of the Groupe Islamique Armé (GIA), a radical Algerian organization reported to be claiming allegiance to Islamic fundamentalism. This chapter does not review those attacks in more detail, nor does it seek to discuss terrorism. Instead, it seeks to place the national will to repress terrorism within the genealogies of denaturalization that we have been tracing. It poses therefore the following questions: How does the fight against terrorism remobilize the discourse on denaturalization, resignify its aims, invent new technologies of government? What are its effects? Whom does it target? And for what purpose? What does it reveal between foreignness, national citizenship, and security?

Paradoxically, despite its decisive resolution regarding denaturalization, the 1996 bill pertaining to the repression of terrorism proved to give it very little attention. First of all, the amendment to article 25 did not even figure in the first version of the parliamentary bill, discussed on December 20, 1995. Initially, the bill solely presented provisions amending the penal code and the code of penal procedures. Obviously, denaturalization was not seen as an evident measure that would improve legislation supporting the fight against terrorism.

The first mention of an amendment to article 25 of the civil code figures in a report by M. Alain Marsaud (1996) written in the name of the commission of constitutional law, submitted to the *Assemblée nationale* on March 13, 1996, so as to inform Parliament's second reading of the bill. Introducing the insertion of a new chapter titled "Provisions Amending the Civil Code," the report reads:

> As announced, Ms. Suzanne Sauvaigo has presented an amendment, adopted by the commission, which creates a new subdivision entitled: "Provisions amending the civil code," comprising an article that expands the scope of Article

25 of the civil code pertaining to the denaturalization of persons convicted for a crime or an offense that qualifies as an act of terrorism. (19)

As the chapter is entirely new to the parliamentary bill, it raises the reader's expectation of finding solid arguments justifying this insertion. Those, however, remain absent from the report. This is troubling for two reasons. First, it bypasses the fact that the new provision is the sole link made between the legislation supporting the fight against terrorism and the civil code. Indeed, all articles contained in the 1996 bill pertaining to the repression of terrorism are provisions amending the penal code or the code of penal procedure, except for the amendment to article 25 of the civil code. In this sense, this amendment re-creates a link between the domain of citizenship and that of penal law.[1] This means that along with the concept of an "act of terrorism," denaturalization practices resurface as a means to preserve the institutions and moral standards of the French Republic, thereby also qualifying as a political decision. Denaturalization's political character further increases with the fact that those targeted are not all citizens who do not behave according to the law, but only those who have obtained French nationality after a process of naturalization. Denaturalization, then, fully participates in the security logics aiming at separating the citizenry from those seen as endangering the political, juridical structure of France as a nation.

Marsaud's formulation of the announced amendment raises further questions as it conveys the impression that measures of denaturalization are very trivial. They prove not to need any arguments. However, this fully discards the fact that, taken at face value, those measures largely contravene the first article of the French Constitution: whereas the latter stipulates the principle of equality before the law, denaturalization produces a condition of citizenship for new nationals that can be revoked in certain situations and thereby does not quite belong to the overall national juridical structure.

Surely, this is a contradiction worth a proper political debate. However, it is striking that the April 18, 1996, parliamentary debate reviewing the commission's report spent hardly any time discussing the new provision. Its brevity makes it worth quoting *in extenso*:

> The second paragraph (1°) of Article 25 is completed by the words: "for a crime or an offense that qualifies as an act of terrorism."
>
> M. the court clerk has the floor.
>
> **M. Alain Marsaud**, *court clerk*. This amendment has been adopted based on Ms. Sauvaigo's initiative.
>
> Perpetrators of a terrorist crime could be deprived of their French nationality if they had acquired it. Such forfeiture of nationality [*déchéance*] is already legislated by Article 25 of the civil code for terrorist crimes leading to a sentence of 5 years or more in prison. Accordingly, the amendment extends the scope of

this article to all terrorist crimes, regardless of the sentence, and to all offenses
of the same nature.

M. the President [of the Assembly]. What is the opinion of the government?

M. the Minister of Justice. I support this amendment because it does not
constitute a novation of principle—it is already registered, indeed, in article 25
of the civil code—but simply a mere extension.

M. the President. I put the amendment number 7 to a vote.

(The amendment is adopted.) (France 1996)

Besides fact that M. Marsaud reiterates the divide between born nationals
and new nationals in his presentation without giving it any specific attention,
the argumentative line is further problematic for several reasons. First, the
amendment finds its legitimacy in a mere rhetorical trick: if the provision
legislates an extension of the scope of article 25, it certainly brings in something that was not yet in place, hence something new; this is the nature of an
amendment. Saying that the provision should be adopted based on the fact
that it is nothing new is thus a rhetorical aberration. Second, the extension the
court clerk is talking about is not even an extension, but rather a completely
new formulation of cases in which the forfeiture of nationality is justified
by law. Indeed, the word "terrorism" had up to that moment never figured
in article 25. Where the court clerk claims that denaturalization was already
legislated "for *terrorist* crimes leading to a sentence of five years of imprisonment or more" (my emphasis), the law in force at that time reads: "for an act
that qualifies as a crime by French law and that leads to a sentence of 5 years
or more in prison." Clearly, the notion of "terrorism" did not initially figure
in article 25, and there is no indication whatsoever that the crimes or offenses
cited must be interpreted as acts of terrorism.

This argumentative slippage in the clerk's report is, at the least, surprising
in the context of the 1996 parliamentary bill pertaining to the repression
of terrorism. For the bill precisely aimed to refine the juridical distinction
between common crimes and offenses and acts of terrorism; it was precisely
because there was a political will to further distinguish between "an act that
qualifies as a crime by French law" and "acts of terrorism" that the bill was
put forward (Masson 1996; Marsaud 1995). Hence, not only is Marsaud's
above-cited argument misleading because it is based on distorted information, but it also contradicts the parliamentary bill and consequently raises
even more questions about its legitimacy.

I suggest that those forces that led to the concept of terrorism's insertion
into article 25 of the French civil code are an expression of the performative power exercised by the concept of terrorism as such. In the following
sections, I substantiate this point while I closely examine some relevant
moments in the governmental debates that led to the definition of "terrorism"

as a juridical category in the French justice system, expressed in the law of September 9, 1986 (France 1986).

DEFINING AN "ACT OF TERRORISM" IN FRENCH JURISDICTION

In France, the creation of a juridical category defining an "act of terrorism" was a direct response to a series of bomb attacks targeting France, and Paris in particular. Claimed by *Action Directe* (a French revolutionary group that considered themselves libertarian communists) and by Hezbollah (a Shi'a Islamic militant group and political party based in Lebanon), the attacks took place between February and September 1986, the bomb attack on the Rue de Rennes on September 17, 1986 in front of the Tati store being the most memorable. The point of this chapter is not to review the details of these attacks,[2] but instead to focus on the politics of the "act of terrorism," paying particular attention to its effects on technologies of governments that both shape and control the divide between people who are desired and those who are not.

Central to the arguments pertaining to the making of the juridical category of "terrorism" was the idea that terrorism is by definition a criminal offense that should be punished accordingly, although it had never been defined as such before the law of September 9, 1986 (Limouzy 1986; Marsaud 1995). These arguments betray a tendency to think of "terrorism" as a self-explanatory term, which makes it arguably unproblematic to categorize in the law. "Terrorism" is then commonly referred to as something that everybody intuitively knows, and as the result of an attack that was claimed as a terrorist act by the perpetrators (Limouzy 1986).

However, the political debates around the 1986 bill pertaining to the fight against terrorism also contain political disagreements regarding what must fall under the definition of an act of terrorism. Terrorist infractions prove not to be solely those self-proclaimed acts of terrorism, as terrorism is not only that which is being defined by terrorists themselves but also that which legislators and the judiciary understand as terrorism.

Although self-proclaimed acts of terrorism were already heterogeneous (ranging from assassination to hostage taking and bomb attacks, to name but a few), the political juridical perception of the term proves to further complicate its meaning. Thus a report by M. Paul Masson (Masson 1996, 10) (senator and rapporteur of the commission of law to the *Sénat*) acknowledged that "the legislator of 1986 had to tackle the problem of the 'missing/unknown definition' [*l'introuvable définition*] of terrorism." Crucial here is the expression of "*introuvable définition*" [missing/unknown definition]. Reading the report further, we see that the expression does not so much refer to the fact that the concept of terrorism had not yet been defined in the law (hence it was missing); rather, it points to the fact that the content of the definition was heterogeneous to such an extent that it made it impossible to express it in terms of a juridical definition. According to Masson, the disturbing heterogeneity was due to the fact that the single term "terrorism" would have referred to extremely diverse facts (such as assassination, theft, and arms dealing), which would put the hierarchy of penalties at risk (10). Furthermore, the creation of a new incrimination such as terrorism, which was not present in the conventions on extradition that France adhered to, could have hindered executing requests for extradition of those involved in a crime of terrorism (10).

These two criteria are interesting in themselves, but the juridical solution that was found for the problem of heterogeneity might say even more regarding what the notion of terrorism is about. Indicative of the performative force exercised by the term "terrorism," the solution was found in a definition of "act of terrorism" (as opposed to the concept of "terrorism" *tout court*) (Masson 1996). "Act of terrorism" was defined according to the following two criteria: 1) it refers to a predetermined crime or offense (such as assassination, hostage taking, or destruction), and 2) it is related to an individual or collective enterprise whose aim is to cause a grave disturbance of the public order by means of intimidation or terror (10).

In the first place, this solution suggests that there is a genuine distinction between "terrorism" and "act of terrorism" because the concept of "terrorism" would not be definable by law, whereas the notion of an "act of terrorism" is. According to the rapporteur's statement, the distinction between "terrorism" and "act of terrorism" would be their degree of heterogeneity. The more heterogeneous, the less a concept is suitable for a juridical definition because juridical definitions must be reasonably known, knowable, and contestable. In itself, the concept of terrorism proved to be too heterogeneous to function as a juridical category and hence required further qualification, which was proposed in calling terrorism as an *act* of terrorism.

However, there is little reason to think that the obvious difference tied to the formulation (the notion of "terrorism" would not necessarily refer to a concrete act, whereas the notion of "act of terrorism" is, in principle, based on a well-defined act) is a genuine difference that solves the problem of the term's degree of heterogeneity. As the following section demonstrates, the semantic field expressed in the juridical definition of "act of terrorism" is in itself intensely heterogeneous. Furthermore, the expression appears to be caught in an affective economy of fear, which both makes use of the heterogeneity at stake and intensifies it.

THE AFFECTIVE ECONOMY BOUND TO
THE CONCEPT OF "TERRORISM"

According to the juridical definition of an act of terrorism, terrorist infractions are not necessarily understood as new forms of violence (such as assassinations, theft, and hostage taking) since they were already known and codified as crimes before "acts of terrorism" came to be codified as a criminal infraction. What is new, according to the law, is their goal and their means, identified as "to cause a grave disturbance of the public order" by means of "intimidation or terror." The juridical solution to the problem of the "*introuvable définition*" of terrorism is thus more a camouflage for the law's incapacity to define the concept of terrorism than a real solution. For the *act* in the expression "act of terrorism" is not that which is terroristic. Terrorism is that which surrounds the act.

This was made explicit by M. Jacques Limouzy (1986), deputy and rapporteur for the commission of law to the *Assemblée nationale* in 1986. He wrote: "It is not in the constitutive elements of the infraction that we can grasp the notion of terrorism, but in the criteria concerning the aim pursued, the consequences of the act, and the means employed." Accordingly, terrorist acts differ from common crimes and offenses in the sense that their effect is more than the mere nature of the act. That is, if assassination were involved, the effect would not solely be the death of an assassinated individual, but also a grave disturbance of the public order accompanied by intimidation or terror. This means that it is not the assassination in itself that is being understood as an act of terrorism, but that which surrounds it in terms of affective effects. Hence, terrorism is not about a criminal infraction; it is not necessarily about an act, but about the affective economy surrounding those acts.

Further characterized by a poor discursive clarity when it comes to what turns a criminal infraction into a terrorist act, the juridical definition of act of terrorism, provided in article 421-1 of the French penal code, reads: "when they are related to an individual or collective enterprise whose aim is to cause a grave disturbance of the public order by means of intimidation or terror" (France 2016). All the main terms in the definition are terms with relative values. For instance, when would an act be considered "related to" an individual or collective enterprise? And what is being understood by "enterprise"? Furthermore, what is the degree of disturbance understood as "a grave disturbance of the public order"? And what is precisely understood by "public order"? Finally, how do we assess feelings such as "intimidation" or "terror"? Clearly, all those aspects rest on a common idea of what it means to be intimidated or terrified, or on what it means to be related to somebody else's activities. Depending on a subjective and contextual appreciation of what they stand for, none of those aspects can be said to be objective criteria.[3]

Such discursive ambiguity is already a sign of the presence of affective values, as it enhances the circulation of emotions in the sense that it broadens the heterogeneous space of language according to which the meaning of words must necessarily remain plural. Furthermore, it brings back Ahmed's work on affective economies (2004a, 2004b). Insisting on the fact that "emotions are not 'in' either the individual or the social, but produce the very surfaces and boundaries that allow the individual and the social to be delineated as if they are objects," Ahmed further states that "it is the very failure of affect to be located in a subject or object that allows it to generate the surfaces of collective bodies" (Ahmed 2004b, 10, 2004a, 128).

Clearly, the ambiguous definition of "act of terrorism" does not locate any specific object (nor any specific subject) as that which can be defined as terrorism. As Julie Alix (2010) explains in her critical study of terrorist incriminations, the penal definition and qualification of terrorism neither targets an act nor a plurality of acts, but an entire criminal phenomenon (11). It is accordingly up to the legislator to express what "terrorist crime" means, which implies that the definition of terrorism is political by nature; defining "terrorism" is not a systematic enterprise based on objective criteria, but instead responds to the pursuit of efficiency (19). This impossibility—or refusal—to define acts of terrorism according to fixed criteria has a particular effect: it turns the notion of terrorism into a discursive formation whose meaning remains intentionally malleable. Consequently, the lack of definition provides a general direction along which the meaning of terrorism can be formed. In turn, such discursive formation performatively contributes to the materialization of a collective body that is aligned against those being labeled as terrorists.

In this context, Didier Bigo's term of "governmentality of unease" (2002) is particularly helpful in further understanding the political and discursive constellation in which the concept of terrorism is ensnared. His analysis especially focuses on the politics of mobility tied to contemporary debates on migration, denouncing the fact that "migration is increasingly interpreted as a security problem" (63). His term, "governmentality of unease," however, is not solely applicable to migration studies, as it refers to a sense of general unease that informs technologies of government in charge of the management of risk and fear (63). "Unease" thus stems from what is perceived as a threat; it refers to those categories that have been associated with what must be kept out of society—"terrorism" being one of the most prominent and determinant ones.

Accordingly, the "governmentality of unease" addresses processes of normalization and abnormalization according to which the positions of individuals are "crossed (or pierced) by the rhizomes of power/resistance relations" (Bigo 2012, 45).[4] Moreover, Bigo's term of "unease" indicates the ways in which security logics play with ambiguity and uncertainty, criteria that result from technologies of government that "work through everyday life" and "[divide] the population into categories of those non desirable, unwanted groups that are to be either integrated in a way of assimilation or to be banned, excluded, removed" (Bigo 2002, 64).

Crucially, the governmentality of unease is also characterized by a lack of legibility when it comes to what distinguishes the desirable from the unwanted groups. Constructed "through a series of actions at a dis-tance/ dis-time," technologies of government involved in processes of normalization and abnormalization both work at a geographical distance and operate at a distance in time (Bigo 2002, 45).[5] Not only do they build on past practices of inclusion and exclusion, they also follow a logic of preemption that, as Marieke de Goede has carefully demonstrated, is central to the fight against terrorism (2012; de Goede and Randalls 2009; de Goede 2008a, 2008b). According to de Goede (2012, 53), preemption "does not endeavor to predict the future, but it pre-mediates the future by mapping and imagining multiple future scenarios that are made actionable in the present." Furthermore, preemptive logics foster a climate of speculative security, and have become technologies of government that operate through suspicion, surprise, and suppleness (53). This has important consequences: while prevention becomes "the new 'doxa' of the solution against a global insecurity and all the different worst-case scenarios" (Bigo 2012, 34), the attention in security logics is no longer concerned with a tangible reality. Instead, it is directed toward an imagined state of insecurity that causes the future to be folded into the here and now. Imagined as a potential threat, the unknown future becomes part of the mechanisms of normalization and abnormalization that define processes of inclusion and exclusion—of which denaturalization is an example.

This concern with preventive measures clearly resonates with those affective economies accounted for in Ahmed's analysis of cultural and political emotions. Following Ahmed's theory, the preemptive logic can now be expressed in terms of positioning the imagined futures as a void through which signs of fear and suspicion circulate in a metonymic slide, producing what Ahmed calls the "rippling effect of emotions" (2004a, 120). Such metonymic slides imply that the future is being connected to a sideways movement as well as to a backward movement according to which emotions "stick" through associations between signs, figures, and objects, while they also connect to the "'absent presence' of historicity" (120).

Ahmed's notion of stickiness primarily refers to the performative effect of a history of articulation and repetitions, according to which a sign comes to evoke other words "which have become intrinsic to the sign through past forms of association" (Ahmed 2004b, 92). It builds on Judith Butler's theory of performativity (1993), understanding performativity as that which "relates to the way in which a signifier, rather than simply naming some-thing that already exists, works to generate that which it apparently names. Performativity is hence about the power of discourse to produce effect through reiteration" (Ahmed 2004b, 92). Furthermore, stickiness involves "a transference of affect" (91). That is, it is about "what objects do to other objects ... but [in] a relation of 'doing' in which there is not a distinction between passive or active" (91). Accordingly, stickiness is an analytical tool that helps identify how the contingency of discursive elements is in itself per-formative (such as with "terrorism" and "new nationals" in article 25 of the civil code): it produces a new reality based on the past associations of signs, which is not necessarily visible but nevertheless participates in the effects of the sign at stake.

Terrorism being the unknown and unknowable threat follows a narrative of uncertainty and crisis that aligns those being labeled as terrorists against the community. While the law proves unable to define it objectively, "terrorism" remains the ultimate category for deciding who needs to be removed from the national environment. Caught in an affective economy of fear and sus-picion, the notion of terrorism disseminates beyond the law. To follow Ahmed's arguments further, the terrorist "could be anywhere and anyone, as a ghostlike figure in the present, who gives us nightmares about the future, as an anticipated future of injury. We see 'him' again and again. Such figures of hate circulate, and indeed accumulate affective value, precisely because they do not have a fixed referent" (2004a, 123).

"ACT OF TERRORISM": STRATEGY
OR PERVERSE TACTIC?

Crucially, as the law has become the space where the notion of an "act of terrorism" is defined, terrorism can no longer solely be understood as those acts claimed to be terrorist acts by those who committed them. Instead, it is now especially defined as those acts that the legislative (and the judiciary) recognize as acts of terrorism following their own definition of it. Sliding across the juridical definition of terrorism, the goals and intention of an act travel from the perpetrators of the act to the legislators: terrorism has become a concept with an affective economy, which is being channeled through the law. First, perpetrators of terrorist acts directly relate to the state and its values as *expressed in the law*, as they challenge the fundamental interests of the state, or its existential conditions. Besides, the affective value of the notion of terrorism, as defined by the state, moves in a very specific way: it travels from state representatives to political social subjects, and not the other way around.[6] In this economy, denaturalization law amplifies the performance of "terrorism" and its metonymic slide: it constructs new nationals as particular citizens and ensnares the notion of nationality and citizenship in the political, juridical language that addresses terrorism.

Accordingly, the juridical definition of terrorism revolves around two different kinds of affective economies: one intrinsic to the semantic content of the law, the other intrinsic to the legislating power. I propose to further the discussion by aligning these affective economies with de Certeau's (1984) understanding of "tactic" and "strategy." I argue that the affective economy intrinsic to the legislating power answers from a strategic logic. In turn, the affective economy intrinsic to the semantic content of the juridical definition of "act of terrorism" operates as a tactic, albeit in a perverse manner.

According to de Certeau (1984), the difference between strategy and tactic "corresponds to two historical options regarding action and security" (38): "strategies pin their hopes on the resistance that the *establishment of a place* offers to the erosions of time; tactics on a clever *utilization of time*, of the opportunity it presents and also of the play that it introduces into the foundations of powers" (39). In this respect, strategies answer from a territorial logic. They are bound to a structural definition of power relations and fastened to a will to secure the territory at stake. Enabling state representatives and the juridical body to control the allocation of terror to those activities that they deem threatening to the public order, the definition of "act of terrorism" is perfectly in line with de Certeau's notion of strategy. Being the legislative response to a certain feeling of insecurity, it establishes a surface of power that helps define and control the national territory.

In turn, de Certeau (1984) understands tactics as the possibility to invest a certain freedom of action within the defined framework of power. As he views it, a tactic is "a calculated action determined by the absence of a proper locus. ... It must vigilantly make use of the cracks that particular conjunctions open in the surveillance of the proprietary powers" (37). Furthermore, de Certeau describes a tactic as "an art of the weak" (37): it is the space available for reappropriation and resistance to those who are subjugated to the established power. In this sense, it is "the space of the Other. Thus it must play on and with a terrain imposed on it and organized by the law of a foreign power" (37).

The juridical definition of the notion of an "act of terrorism," however, reveals that tactics are not necessarily "an art of the weak," as they can also be the maneuvers of those individuals who are in power. Crucially, the discursive ambiguity proper to the definition of an "act of terrorism" remains in the hands of legislators and magistrates. That is, although the discursive ambiguous space identified in the definition provides a clear space where the allocation of meaning is negotiated again and again, those who have access to those negotiations are precisely those who define the boundaries of power. Hence, while the form of the definition (that is, the structure of the law) shapes a surface and a frame of power, the discursive looseness of its content makes it possible for those in power to expand the surface's boundaries at will.

Strategies and Tactics in Practice

The effects of such interaction between strategy and tactics can be further interrogated by looking at the ways in which the term "terrorism" performs throughout the judicial body. Those case studies remain tendentious, however, and especially difficult to address critically in the wake of attacks that have cost the lives of hundreds of people. After all, terrorism *is* an affective concept, and sometimes the emotions that it arouses seem too close to abolish the distance of scholarly analysis. In fact, addressing such cases from a critical perspective first and foremost demands looking at them in a "naïve" way, that is, trying to set aside the dominant associations and connotations that circulate with the term and to allow its "failed" associations to become visible.[7] J. Halberstam (2011, 12) argues that naïve readings "may in fact lead to a different set of knowledge practices." Accordingly, their use participates in the endeavor to demystify institutionary language by "refusing to acquiesce to dominant logics of power and discipline and as a form of critique" (88). In the context of terrorism, such naïve readings involve the risk of being read as siding against the state and endorsing terrorism. Although there are many ways of challenging and resisting the refrain of "either you are with us or against us" that politicians and media collectively adopted after 9/11, the slogan's infiltrating performative force compels me to make it unequivocally explicit that although my analysis contains a critique regarding the way institutional voices have pushed terrorism into the uncanny space of hyperrecognition and voicelessness simultaneously, it does not intend in any way whatsoever to stage terrorism as that which must be rescued. Instead, what is at stake is to recognize that by placing an ill-defined concept in the space of that which must be expelled as abject from society by all accessible means, legislative and judiciary powers participate in the circulation of an affective economy that sticks to the bodies of those who are labeled as terrorists. Producing an abnormal category with no clear semantic content, the legislature and the judiciary establish a surface of power whose boundaries are highly political, as they result from both strategic and tactical maneuvers.

Methodologically speaking, investigating a contemporary case that involves terrorism adds an element of unease to the research when it comes to gathering an archive of primary sources. Most of all, the researcher needs to negotiate with the politics of secrecy, applying both to information relating to or dealing with security matters and jurisdictional procedures (France 2018). Such politics of secrecy does not mean, however, that no primary sources can be gathered. Yet the means of research are less conventional than visiting institutionalized archives. Instead of researching documents that have already been classified and ordered according to a system of knowledge and administration, the researcher is especially dependent on what can be found on the Internet, the latter providing an extremely fuzzy yet openly accessible source of documentation.

Surely, all archival research goes hand in hand with the imperative of reflecting on the history of the consulted documents. Archives are the result of multiple processes of selection, starting by the selective process resulting from the art of writing (Goody 1986). All written documents bear the trace of an event; however, all events have not been recorded. Additionally, archives build on a politics of power and knowledge, being at the same time "the law of what can be said" and "that which … defines … the system of its enunciability" (Foucault 1982, 145, 146). In other words, while selecting that which may be remembered, archives also produce systems through which the documents are organized and consigned.[8] Such systems inevitably interfere with practices of reading and interpretation, as they participate in the knowledge practices that lay behind the foundational logic of any archive.

If the Internet bypasses many of those administrative systems according to which a document may or may not be made available for readers like you and me, its fuzziness brings in the difficulty of knowing how to assess the quality of information gathered around one's object of research. In charge of filtering and selecting information, the researcher is now the one who, besides developing practices of reading and interpretation, also has the duty to elaborate a primary system of knowledge practices. The boundaries of such a system go beyond official narratives of administrated knowledge (that is, information that is provided by official parties such as the government, the judiciary system, or validated scientific sources), but they nevertheless remain confined to that which the semi-public domain of the web offers.[9]

One of the cases I have looked into is that of Djamel Beghal prior to his denaturalization in 2006. My choice for analysis of his case was partly made because a considerable amount of information concerning his trial was made available through various open digital channels. These range from media reports and informative blogs, to judiciary documents such as administrative jurisprudence from the *Conseil d'État* and jurisprudence from the European Court of Human Rights (both openly accessible), to leaked diplomatic cables coming from an anonymous source inside the American embassy in Paris and made available by WikiLeaks, as well as to a transcript of the Accusation Act pronounced by the Court of Appeal in his case, anonymously uploaded to the

Web. In addition, the ministerial decree of denaturalization was made available by the Governmental Portal for Legal and Administration Information upon request.

Without question, the narratives these documents provide remain but a fragment of the entire case, especially knowing that in the meantime, Beghal was identified as the mentor of those who perpetrated the Paris attacks in 2015. Although in principle, any case study remains based on partial information, if we acknowledge the selective processes applying to historical sources, the complexity of this particular case must be stressed to make it clear that it would require further work to treat it as a full case study. The question of Beghal's role in the 2015 attacks is a question that needs to be addressed on its own, but that remains outside the scope of this analysis. Focusing on those processes that led to Beghal's denaturalization in 2006, the following analysis concentrates on the discursive dynamics observable in the documents available in order to reflect on the ways in which strategy and tactic interact in the realm of governmental power.

An abridged overview of the juridical facts of the case reads: on March 15, 2005, Beghal was convicted of terrorist conspiracy and sentenced to ten years imprisonment, a decision that was confirmed by the Court of Appeal on December 14, 2005. A year later, on December 23, 2006, a ministerial decree for the forfeiture of his French nationality was made against him based on the first paragraph of article 25 of the civil code (i.e., the clause that codifies the forfeiture of nationality for acts of terrorism). The decision was confirmed by the *Conseil d'État* on September 26, 2007, despite an appeal from Beghal's defense. On September 19, 2007, Beghal faced a ministerial decree of expulsion to Algeria. Despite his renewed appeal, the sentence of expulsion was approved by the Administrative Court on May 26, 2009, which pushed Beghal to solicit help from the European Court of Human Rights on May 27, 2009. The latter blocked his deportation, based on a fear deemed reasonable that Beghal would be exposed to systematic torture if deported. Accordingly, Beghal remained in detention on French territory. On the informal blog dedicated to his release from detention ("Djamel Beghal: Terroriste Ou Prisonier d'opinion?" 2013), he himself maintains his innocence of the charges raised against him.[10]

While the accusation act publically declared Beghal to be a terrorist by convicting him of terrorist conspiracy, "terrorism" had already begun being associated with Beghal's person the moment he became a suspected terrorist. Placed in pretrial detention, Beghal was subjected to a thorough investigation carried out by Islamic/international terrorism investigating judges Jean-François Ricard and Jean-Louis Brugière. Following the law of September 9, 1986, they represented the special investigation unit of the *Tribunal de Grande Instance* in Paris, specialized in the fight against terrorism and attacks that undermine the security of the state and therefore responsible for carrying out all investigations pertaining to cases in which terrorism might be involved. Producing a metonymic slide and its accompanying rippling effect, such specialized investigating units produce an *a priori* discursive associability between the concept of terrorism and the suspect's body and deeds: while specialized investigating judges investigate their cases according to their specialized knowledge of terrorism, they frame the subject of investigation in specific terms, thereby activating a certain realm of knowledge politics. Framing a subject in terms of a potential terrorist is indeed performative as it is an "act with consequences": it opens realms of possibilities in terms of judicial procedures that differ from other kinds of investigations.

In terms of strategy and tactic, the investigation procedure is a clear instance in which the concept of terrorism is caught in a strategic gesture. Positioned as a threat to France's security, the suspect is by definition ensnared in an economy of fear and suspicion according to which the judiciary power controls the allocation of terror to what it deems threatening to the public order. Accordingly, as a discursive enterprise, the investigation contributes to the social constitution of the suspect as a terrorist, as well as to the establishment of a surface of power whose purpose is to secure the national territory. Yet, just as it was the case in the realm of the legislative power, the judiciary's power does not solely operate in a strategic way. On several occasions, the formulation of the judiciary's conclusions reveals the extent to which their strategic power is also based on a tactical maneuver according to which their frame of power expands beyond its own limits. For instance, the accusation act by the Court of Appeal (*Cour d'Appel de Paris*) reads:

> The Court observes that even if there is no solid evidence in the file that Beghal meant to attack American interests in Paris, an embassy or cultural center, unless we count a statement made by Beghal Djamel before the UAE investigators, which was received in non-conformity with the rights to defense and thus cannot be held against the defendant, the fact remains that the involvement of the person concerned in the most radical Islamist movements, supported by Al Qaeda of which it has been proved that their aim is to destabilize occidental regimes supporting the United States and Israel, has been revealed by the elements gathered by the investigation and instruction recalled by the Tribunal and the Court. (Cour d'Appel de Paris 2005)

The strategic maneuver is especially visible in the extraordinary formulation of "even if the actual evidence of a planned attack ... is not reported within procedure ..., the fact remains that ...." Such a formulation points to a specific discursive circulation: the meaning of the criteria of turning someone into a terrorist shifts. Indicative of an affective economy that sticks, the label of terrorism emerges as the effect of a history of articulation and repetitions that produces a transference of affect according to which "terrorism" becomes associated with Beghal as a person. First, while the expression of "terrorism" is not literally mentioned in the court's sentence, the notion is carried by phrases such as "attack," "most radical Islamist movements," "Al Qaida," and "aims to destabilize occidental regimes." Recurrent in the most common narratives applying to the fight against terrorism, these phrases carry the notion of terrorism with them. In other words, their use "[reopens] past associations that allow some bodies to be read as the cause of 'our hate,' or as 'being' hateful" (Ahmed 2004a, 120). Simultaneously, the concept of terrorism moves sideways as it slides between figures through the performative association of terrorist signs and Beghal's identity. While the court says they lack evidence of the conspiracy to attack American interests in Paris, the lack of evidence slides into pole position. The court's statement in itself produces the performative evidence that Beghal might indeed be a terrorist.

Such performative power and tactical maneuvering of the judiciary is made even more visible when one reads a classified diplomatic cable by a secretary's aide working at the American Embassy in Paris (American Embassy Paris 2005).[11] The cable reports on French antiterrorism policy strategies. One of the points mentions a remark by investigating judge Ricard concerning Beghal's trial, which reads as follows:

> He said his office depended significantly upon its reputation within the French justice system, which tends to give the terrorism investigating judges the benefit of the doubt. (As an example, Ricard said that the proof against recently convicted Djamel Beghal and his accomplices, accused of plotting to bomb the US Embassy, would not normally be sufficient to convict them, but he believed his office was successful because of their reputation.)

The fact that this cable was classified comes as no surprise, be it only for the fact that it reports on the investigation judge's comments on Beghal's trial (which goes against the confidentiality of investigations), not to mention the content of its message: that an investigation office may bypass the rules of justice simply "because of their reputation." And yet it does nothing but confirm what was already implicitly legible in the public report by the Court of Appeal and in the way "terrorism" had been juridically defined. For instance, the fact that "normal" standards of justice do not necessarily hold when it comes to terrorism (the accusations against Beghal "would not normally be sufficient to convict him"; "the French justice system ... tends to give the terrorism investigating judges the benefit of the doubt") was already stated by the court in terms that can be paraphrased as "despite the fact that there is no evidence, it remains a fact that Beghal belongs to the terrorists." Furthermore, Ricard's statement on his office's reputation confirms the hypothesis that the juridical definition of terrorism allows for the authorities to tactically shift the boundaries of power in which they operate.

Convicted of terrorist conspiracy, Beghal, who was originally an Algerian national and who had come to France in 1987 to study (he married a French woman in 1990 and acquired French nationality in 1993, and had three children, all of whom possess French nationality) was stripped of his French nationality. His case fit the boundaries of denaturalization law: as a new national, Beghal fell into the category of "national by acquisition" understood to represent a fundamental threat to the nation. Dated December 23, 2006, the decree of denaturalization symbolically de-linked Beghal from the French political community, thereby institutionalizing him as an illegitimate citizen. His potential contribution to the 2015 Paris attacks, however, painfully raises the question of the efficacy of denaturalization as a security measure. Despite the emotional responses that such attacks arouse, it remains important to ask what is then at stake in denaturalization practices, and what the link between denaturalization and "terrorism" produces.

What is striking is not so much the appearance of the juridical definition of the crime of terrorism in French law; the quality of the 1980s attacks might well have justified such a definition in light of the principle of legality in criminal law. The point of this chapter is rather to raise questions about the link produced between the concept and definition of "terrorism" and the realm of citizen rights. At the crossroads of politics of security and national citizenship, denaturalization is a technology of government used to ostracize citizens whose inscription within the national community is perceived as a threat to the interest of the state. Surely, the notion of citizenship has always rested on exclusion and divisions between insiders and outsiders, but the quick and unreflective insertion of the concept of "terrorism" in the language of denaturalization—and hence in the civil code—reveals a tremendous and highly ambiguous increase in the state's capacity to make foreign those who are prosecuted in the name of the nation's security. Thereby, denaturalization is no longer, as Patrick Weil states it (2008, 244), simply a "reserve of sovereignty that allows the state to intervene in exceptional cases." Instead, the affective economy bound to the concept of terrorism stresses the problem of having such a structural "reserve of sovereignty" when the criteria for such a reserve are in themselves a way for governmental powers to revise the limit of their authority *ad hoc*. In other words, the criteria for defining the terms of an "exceptional intervention" are in themselves another "reserve of sovereignty." Such "reserves of sovereignty" are therefore potentially infinite and betray the presence of a chronic "totalitarian infection" (Arendt 1973) in French politics of national citizenship.

NOTES

1. This link was already present in the French Revolution period, but has been camouflaged since World War I, as denaturalization came to be inscribed in the civil code. During the French Revolution, and as discussed in chapter 4, criminal law was the framework of the new public order, its primary objective being to defend the institutions and new Republican values (Simonin 2008, 39). While the structure of new political and juridical institutions believed to be capable of delivering a universalized society, criminal law was the means to get rid of the "bad citizens" by means of the new penalty of civic degradation, which struck by inflicting temporary indignity on the citizen who had dishonored himself (Simonin 2008, 40). In effect, and as demonstrated throughout the chapters, the political link between denaturalization and the penal code has never fully been broken, denaturalization being this instrument for the state to make foreign (both literally and politically) those who are perceived as a threat; from nationals by acquisitions born in an enemy nation for the period of World War I, to Communists in the 1930s, to Jews and political dissidents in World War II.

2. For a thorough analysis of the attacks, I refer to Didier Bigo's 1991 article "Les Attentats de 1986 en France."

3. The ambiguity of those questions finds illustration in the Tarnac case of terrorism labeling, a case in which a number of left-wing activists were arrested in the rural French village of Tarnac in 2008 on a charge of "pre-terrorism," an accusation linked to acts of sabotage on France's TGV rail system (Critchley 2011). As described by Simon Critchley, their arrest was part of "Nicholas Sarkozy's reactionary politics of fear" (171), and the labeling of "pre-terrorism" followed a "surprising juridical imagination" (172).

4. The terms "normalization" and "abnormalization" refer to Foucault's terminology, which points at the relation between a system of norms and a system of law. According to Foucault (2007a, 56), technologies of normalization are not intrinsic to the law, but "develop from and below the law, in its margins and maybe even against it."

5. One of the most striking examples of such geographical distance is the operation and control of drones. Drones are unmanned combat aerial vehicles that are mainly used by the United States and the UK in their fight against terrorism. In 2013, it became public knowledge that drones were concomitant with denaturalization practices. So the *Independent* published an article by Chris Woods, Alice K. Ross, and Oliver Wright titled "British Terror Suspects Quietly Stripped of Citizenship . . . then Killed by Drones" on February 28, 2013. The Bureau of Investigative Journalism (an independent nonprofit organization aiming at "educating the public and the media on both the realities of today's world and the value of honest reporting") devoted a whole dossier to drone policies in the UK and their relation to practices of denaturalization, to be consulted on their website under the tag of "secret justice." Likewise, the *Washington Post* published an article by Dylan Matthews entitled "Everything You Need to Know about the Drone Debate" on March 8, 2013, in which he uncovers how drones are being unlawfully used by the US government, and how they also lethally

target US citizens. For the sake of analytical focus, I will not analyze these cases in detail here since they do not directly apply to the French case at hand. However, a comparative study of French practices of denaturalization and the use of drone policies in the UK and United States would be of great interest in further research.

6. Some may argue that the same may be said of robbers with respect to the state's ambiguous definition of "property" as "the right to enjoy and dispose of things in the most absolute way" (France 1804). The specificity of the affective economy of an "act of terrorism," however, lies in its influence on the public and the collective spheres, as opposed to the personal.

7. I refer here to J. Halberstam's understanding of failure, described as "a way of refusing to acquiesce to dominant logics of power and discipline" and as "a form of critique" (2011, 88). Furthermore, Halberstam notes that "[as] a practice, failure recognizes that alternatives are embedded already in the dominant and that power is never total or consistent; indeed failure can exploit the unpredictability of ideology and its indeterminate qualities" (88).

8. The process of selection might differ radically among public archives, private archives, and archives of clandestine organizations, for instance.

9. I am well aware that the web is neither exactly public, nor free from practices of governmental control. What I refer to as "semi-public domain" is the space in which an unquantifiable amount of information is made available for consultation to anyone searching the Internet without making use of any special infiltrating techniques.

10. The various sources commenting on his trial also mention that Beghal maintained his innocence before the judge.

11. Next to WikiLeaks, the cable has been further publically reiterated and discussed by *Le Monde* in Smolar's article "WikiLeaks: On How Washington Assesses the Fight Against Terrorism in France" (Smolar 2010). Subsequently, the *Le Monde* article was quoted on numerous occasions by bloggers.

Chapter 9

The Twenty-First-Century Struggles
over Denaturalization

When I first encountered denaturalization in the context of the 2010 riots in Grenoble, security immediately appeared as a main theme. Presented as a security measure that would prevent future urban riots, denaturalization was exposed as a technology of government that would alleviate a supposedly generalized feeling of insecurity.[1] I then thought, before embarking on doing archival research, that denaturalization was fairly new and belonged to the post-9/11 security apparatus. I was wrong. This genealogy shows that Sarkozy's vision of denaturalization was nothing new in French nationality politics. It was neither the first nor the last political proposition of its kind. On the contrary, the 2010 debate sheds light on what I have shown to be a deep-seated political principle: deep-seated in the sense that it belongs to those major moments of crises that have shaped the institutions of citizenship and nationality in France. The issue was still resonating with security measures presented by the socialist government elected after Sarkozy left office. Denaturalization is a technology of government that transcends right and left wings when it comes to governing citizens whose inscription within the national community is perceived as a threat to the interests of the state.

Presented in systematic relation to feelings of national, regional, or global insecurity, the concept of security exercises a powerful performative framework that drives denaturalization as a technology of government. As this genealogy has exposed, amendments to denaturalization law were systematically brought about when insecurity was a major political concern—from World Wars I and II to the current war on terror. The politics of denaturalization is thus an expression of the "securitization" of national citizenship.[2] As Buzan, Wæver, and Wilde (1998) explain, when an issue is "securitized," it means that "the issue is presented as an existential threat, requiring emergency measures and justifying actions outside the normal bounds of political procedure" (24). When studying denaturalization, we see the extent to which "['security'] is the move that takes politics beyond the established rules of the game and frames the issue either as a special kind of politics or as above politics" (23). While governments legitimize denaturalization by framing it in terms of security and emergency, the rhetoric of security exercises a performative power as it contributes to the realization of new, special regulations; security first and foremost appears as a pretext used to legitimize denaturalization. This was most plainly observed in the context of World War II (see part II). Denaturalization was presented as an unavoidable measure to enhance national security in the context of war (France 1939), but it did not, however, figure among the list of measures taken against individuals deemed to be a threat to the national defense and to public security (France 1941d).

What we saw, then, is that denaturalization rhetoric reproduces, but also distorts, the classical security dilemma according to which the demand for protection against existential danger undermines other fundamental rights (Guillaume and Huysmans 2013, 9). Presented as a security measure, practices of denaturalization relegate equality and freedom, as it makes some citizens lose their rights for the sake of the community as a whole. Here, the language of denaturalization echoes Bonnie Honig's (2002) statements:

> Although we may sometimes persecute people because they are foreign, the deeper truth is that we almost always make foreign those whom we persecute. Foreignness is a symbolic marker that the nation attaches to the people we want to disavow, deport, or detain because we experience them as a threat. The distinction between who is part of the nation and who is an outsider is not exhausted nor even finally defined by working papers, skin color, ethnicity, or citizenship. Indeed, it is not an empirical line at all; it is a symbolic one, used for political purposes.

Surely, the language of denaturalization turns into foreigners those persons who are prosecuted in the name of the state's security. It conflates concerns about immigration with security issues. It literally makes foreign those being prosecuted through empirically defined administrative categories (e.g., national identity and citizenship). And most importantly, denaturalization makes foreign those who are constructed as a threat beyond any empirical line: it is used for political purposes, enabling governments to constantly review, adapt, and rework the definition of the "threatening" subject. Practices of denaturalization thus sustain a specific, and adaptable, politics of repression.

As Patrick Weil explains (2008, 244), such politics of repression is constitutive of the liberalism of French nationality law. He observes that the definitive introduction of denaturalization into French law in 1927 coincides with a moment "when the French legislature was choosing to open the door to widespread naturalization and to accept dual nationality" (240). This leads him to see denaturalization "not at all alien to liberal nationality law but rather constitutive of it" (240). As such, denaturalization "remains as a reserve of sovereignty that allows the state to intervene in exceptional cases" (244). This genealogy confirms that denaturalization is ingrained in French nationality politics, but it also emphasizes the problem of having a structural "reserve of sovereignty" when the criteria for such a reserve are in themselves a way for governmental powers to revise the limits of their authority *ad hoc*.

In sum, while denaturalization is about making foreign those who are perceived as a threat, it also endows the state with increasing means to decide who is worthy of being a citizen and who must be subjected to prosecution in the name of national security. In the context of Olympe de Gouges's trial (chapter 3), we saw the extent to which the formal demarcation line between "friend" and "foe" boiled down to a subjective, contingent appreciation of "consenting love for the *patrie*." We witnessed a discursive process of difference and displacement according to which de Gouges's love for the *patrie* was not recognized as love but was instead reappropriated by the Revolutionary Court as proof of her treason against the revolutionary project. Her texts were presented as threatening to such an extent that she herself had to die for her words. Ironically, the emerging "democratic" community saw no other way to protect itself than to get rid of those questioning its legitimacy. In a similar vein, denaturalization was used against those who resisted the Vichy government during World War II (chapter 6). Nowadays, we are faced with the notion of "terrorism," a word whose semantic content remains opaque to such an extent that it enables governmental powers to shift the boundaries of their legitimate authority, making the borders of nationality more mobile than ever (chapter 8).

Without doubt, terrorism is a grave and critical reality that must be dealt with, with the most careful and serious considerations. This book is not against counterterrorism measures as such. What it questions, however, are the effects of using nationality and citizenship as "weapons" against actors who have been labeled as a threat. In a time when the securitization of borders and identities has become an all-encompassing political framework, denaturalization's genealogical exposure compels us to question what is really at stake in the ways in which, today, states continue to deploy it as a technology of government. At this point it is worth examining the most recent developments in terms of denaturalization legislation in France.

DENATURALIZATION'S PRESENT HISTORY

The Paris attacks on January 7–9, 2015, and on November 13, 2015, revealed a pan-European (more generally Western) symptom: denaturalization has resurfaced across Europe and the United States and beyond, and is presented as yet another security measure in the ever-increasing array of counter-terrorism policies. Among others, France, Britain, the Netherlands, Australia, and the United States consider denaturalizing citizens who leave their countries to fight with rebellious divisions abroad, for example in Syria.

In France, a number of bills were submitted to the *Assemblée nationale*, not after, but before the Paris attacks of 2015: one in April 2013, presented by deputy Philippe Meunier (and colleagues), requesting denaturalization by decree, with the simple advice of the *Conseil d'État* (Supreme Court), of all bi-nationals taking up arms against military or police forces (France 2013); one in May 2014, presented by deputy Jacques Bompard, requesting a broadening of article 25 of the civil code to allow the denaturalization of rebels fighting in Syria (France 2014a); one in June 2014, presented by deputy Lionnel Luca (and colleagues), requesting the possibility to denaturalize "all French citizens" who "enroll in jihadist movements or engage in acts constituting an act of terrorism" (France 2014b).

The political will to expand the scope of denaturalization practices was most visible, however, in the wake of the November 2015 terrorist attacks. In the few days following the attacks, the topic was already on the lips of mourning citizens and politicians alike, figuring most notably in the presidential speech before Parliament on November 16, 2015, in Versailles. Bringing together both chambers of Parliament, the *Assemblée nationale* and the *Sénat*, the speech indicated the gravity of the situation: in France, Parliament only gathers following a presidential decree. It may happen in the event of revisions to the Constitution, of authorizing the admission of a country to the European Union, and of a presidential address. The opening of the presidential address on November 16, 2015, three days after the attacks, set the tone: "France is at war," declared the president (Hollande 2015). Expanding within the established framework of war, the president's speech explained why such a declaration of war would be justified, and presented the government's strategic plan in response to the attack.

One of the particular arguments presented was ensnared in a rhetorical move endeavoring to bring security at the core of democratic life, yet finding resources in one of the most unexpected symbolic places: "Democracy has the capacity to react," claimed the president. He continued: "The Declaration of the Rights of Man and of the Citizen affirms in its article 2 that safety and resistance to oppression are fundamental rights. Accordingly, we must exercise those rights" (Hollande 2015, 18:54). Such a rhetorical move is serious enough. A telling example of the extent to which frameworks of security may fundamentally pervert some of the most fundamental bases of legal protection, Hollande's argument misfired as it appropriated the symbolic authority of human rights where such authority had no place whatsoever. Most certainly, human rights have never been declared with the intention of legitimizing any declaration of war; they were declared to protect citizens from abusive practices of power and authority, aiming "at the pursuance of the interest of human beings" (Arosemena 2014, 261). Accordingly, the content of Hollande's argument can only be dismissed, but its rhetorical effect remains: it aligns with the security framework established from the start and links security to democratic concerns, shaping a frame of exception that contained the arguments to come.

Hollande's misuse of human rights may make his argument theoretically problematic, yet its proclamation resounded as an exacerbation of the political will to install an order of exception; his proclamation seemed to imply that the attacks' exceptional circumstances might have justified an exceptional reading of the symbolic authority of protective rights. To be clear: no single exceptional circumstance may ever justify an exceptional and perverted reading of protective rights. Yet indeed, the arguments that followed first of all put forward Hollande's intention to declare a state of emergency for three months, and to revise the conditions of its possibility, within the Constitution. Furthermore, they also presented the presidential will to revise the conditions under which denaturalization could take place. Hollande declared:

This revision of the Constitution must be complemented by further measures. Denaturalization. Denaturalization should not lead to statelessness. But we must be able to denaturalize an individual convicted for undermining the fundamental interests of the nation or for an act of terrorism, even if that individual was born French. I did say even if that individual was born French. Whenever that individual beneficiates from another nationality. (2015, 23:06)

The repetition in Hollande's argumentation ("I did say even if that individual was born French") marks the gravity of the measure pertaining to the governmental will to expand the scope of denaturalization practices beyond the effective distinction between born nationals and new nationals. In line with the bills submitted to the *Assemblée nationale* in 2013 and 2014, Hollande's proposition goes further than the already existing legislation. In the past, denaturalization would be pronounced with the consent of the *Conseil d'État*; it would only apply to nationals by acquisition; and denaturalization would only be pronounced within a certain limited time period beginning at the individual's naturalization.[3] In Hollande's proposition, just as in the bills submitted to Parliament in 2013, the distinction between French-born nationals and new nationals had disappeared, and the politics of denaturalization would apply to *all* French citizens.[4]

CHIMERA OF EQUALITY AND POLITICAL STRUGGLES

In light of this study's critique of the differentiating principle observed in the French politics of nationality, the political will to abolish the distinction between born nationals and new nationals in denaturalization practices is a paradoxical development. After all, my critique is implicitly arguing for equality, and the devil's advocate might suggest that it would be illogical not to welcome such equalization of denaturalization criteria. These political propositions thus seem to question some of my premises: that the main problem of denaturalization would be its breach with the principle of equality before the law, since the law treats citizens differently if they are "born" or "new" nationals. Yet my plea toward equality is not solely a matter of equality between citizens before the law. Although I am arguing for equality, my critique is especially aimed at the erosion of some of the most fundamental principles of democracy. The principle of equality before the law belongs to them, but is not the only one, and especially not if stripping rights from citizens becomes a means to substantiate it. Equally important is a reasonable predictability of the political and juridical system. Normative criteria need to be known, knowable, and contestable. Investigating the genealogy of denaturalization has revealed that criteria informing denaturalization decrees are especially affective, adaptable, and opaque.

Accordingly, we need to look at what these bills and proposed constitutional reforms produce. Are the authors really proposing to institutionalize a more equal treatment among French citizens? Or, instead, is the state plainly increasing its room to maneuver to the detriment of its citizens?

Far from constituting a democratic improvement, the equalization of denaturalization criteria instigates an apparent contradiction. While denaturalization is presented as a measure against "terrorist" threats, denaturalization practices as such represent a threat against fundamental democratic principles: they reactivate the "totalitarian infection" (Arendt 1973) diagnosed in the context of World War II (chapter 7). Besides the regressive "reserve of sovereignty" characteristic of denaturalization law, studies have also shown that counterterrorism measures (taken by the Financial Action Task Force, for instance) fail to effectively target terrorist organizations; instead, they affect those fighting for democratic principles, such as human rights organizations at work in the regions identified as terrorist headquarters (Broekhoven 2013; Hayes 2012). By extension, the denaturalization of those going to fight in

Syria gives absolutely no guarantee that terrorists will stop traveling; nor does denaturalization suggest that jihadist movements will stop attracting our neighbors. Instead, as the most recent political propositions on denaturalization further demonstrate, rhetorical arguments in favor of denaturalization especially seek to increase the state's capacity to make foreign those who are prosecuted in the name of the nation's security; we have no guarantee that the prosecuted will not be those involved in the recognition of rights for less recognizable forms of political subjectivity.

Christiane Taubira's Act

Former minister of justice, Christiane Taubira, was one of the public voices to openly and powerfully address the fact that denaturalization represents a threat against fundamental democratic principles. One of the few women of color to have ever sat in the French government, Taubira is known for her battles geared to the ideal of the republican mantra of equality. Based on her disagreement with Hollande's proposition to include denaturalization in the Constitution, she resigned as minister of justice on January 22, 2016. "Sometimes, resisting is staying; sometimes resisting is leaving. By fidelity to oneself, to us. For the last word on ethics and law," she wrote on Twitter when announcing her resignation (2016c). Her act to resign resounded worldwide as a political claim, making unusually salient the extent to which the stakes of denaturalization are high. As she explained to the press before leaving the ministry:

> I'm leaving the administration, based upon a major political disagreement. I am choosing to be faithful to myself, to my commitments, to my battles, to my relationship with others; faithful to *us*, in line with my understanding of what *us* means. The terrorist danger is a grave and critical threat, unpredictable; but we have learned to hunt it down, and we have given ourselves the means to do so. We know how to fight it and we have shown the extent to which we are ready to eradicate it. But I believe that we must concede it no single victory, neither a military one, nor a diplomatic one, nor a political one, nor a symbolic one. (2016a)

Taubira's resignation performs several functions. A prominent public voice, her decision to resign such a key political role is first of all a symbolic and political act. By actively countering the political will to broaden denaturalization practices from her position as minister of justice, she confirms that denaturalization is ensnared in those political dynamics that form and reform the contours of the nation's juridical political community. The emphasis on "us" in her resignation speech clearly refers to the national community that

she represents. Her role as minister of justice is crucial here: being the one
with the task to safeguard the legitimacy of the national juridical system and
juridical norms, she bears the authority to safeguard symbolic borders of the
national community for which she is responsible. Communal symbols are
neither self-explanatory nor innocent, she suggests. By acknowledging that
political juridical boundaries are dependent upon discursive interpretations,
she recenters the definition of national community into a frame of knowledge
politics.

Taubira's resignation speech also performs by resisting the affective
dynamics common to security rhetoric. She admits the reality of the security
crisis that France was facing in the wake of the 2015 series of attacks, but
instead of siding with the general argumentative line using the framework
of insecurity to legitimize denaturalization practices, she hints at a series of
new arguments to acknowledge that in practice, denaturalization practices
are different from those pragmatic technologies of government deployed to
hunt down terrorism. Instead, she alludes to denaturalization as a symbolic
gesture, which, as she suggests, is politically detrimental, as it in fact might
even concede terrain to those instigating terror into the population. Her
understanding of denaturalization as symbol politics is further developed
in her essay "*Murmures à la Jeunesse*" [Murmuring to the Youth] that she
published in the wake of her resignation (2016b). There, she explicitly qualifies denaturalization as symbol politics (40); there is nothing in denaturalization practices that has proven to be effective in the fight against terrorism and
its ineffectiveness is a unanimously recognized fact (40). Denaturalization is
indeed a symbol: the symbol of making foreign those being prosecuted in the
name of the state's security. Yet, siding with a view on language that acknowledges the performative force of signs, Taubira stresses that, far from being
innocent, symbol politics has far-reaching consequences. She writes:

> Sometimes, the symbol is all-encompassing. … The symbol connects. It puts
> together. … It is semiotic, in other words it is a sign and carries meaning. This
> meaning is implicit because it refers back to a national history and a national
> writing. It carries the meaning of something acquired, hovering above us. It is
> charged with energy. A symbol is therefore never banal. It has a social function
> and an ethical dimension. (41–42)

In line with Butler's qualification of performative language as "an act with
consequences" (1997, 6), and resonating with Morrison's poetic lines "We do
language. That may be the measure of our lives" (1993), Taubira's acknowledgment that symbols are profound social actors opens up a space of debate
about the social and ethical consequences of denaturalization law. According
to her, the social-performative consequences of symbols as markers of a

community's boundaries raise the fundamental question of whom the symbol really targets. Referring to Hollande's proposition to broaden the scope of denaturalization to all individuals with dual nationality convicted for a crime or offense constituting a fundamental threat to the nation, she asks: "To whom does the symbol of denaturalization for born nationals speak?" (42). Her answer, anchored in a down-to-earth consideration of the actors involved, demonstrates her awareness that language produces an affective rippling effect: "Since [the symbol of denaturalization] does not speak to the terrorists—if we agree that it is not conceivable to imagine them dialoguing with the nation—who does become, by default, the recipient of the message? Those who share with the targeted criminals, by mere coincidence, the fact of being bi-nationals; nothing else" (42). In effect, Taubira points here at the discursive consequences of denaturalization law: instituting a differentiating principle within the understanding of national citizenship, denaturalization law provokes a social and political awareness that equality before the law is relative. Indeed, denaturalization implies that "all [people] are equal, but some [people] are more equal than others" (Orwell 1989, 97).

It is this symbol of differentiation that Taubira refuses to stand for. As she further explains, such a differentiating symbol produces "a consciousness of target for those being concerned, even though not directly addressed; [it generates] an alarming insecurity for their children; and for all people attached to the republican construction of the right to nationality, [it arouses] the feeling of a tremor shaking the essential" (2016b, 46). Surely, her conception of the republican ideal of the right to nationality is here idealized and doesn't take into account the genealogy of difference and repression that permeates the entire history of France as a nation-state. Nonetheless, her motives to resign appear as a rare prominent, public, political voice against denaturalization, which precisely denounces the systemic differentiating principle enshrined in denaturalization practices.

Considering the force of conviction emanating from her act, I am left wondering about her absence of open critique about the *current* law on denaturalization. We can only speculate about the reasons of her silence; it might simply be a battle that she chose not to fight, based on the current political climate that seems to be everything but ready to give up on already established measures framed in terms of security and counterterrorism. After all, the history of denaturalization law in France precisely demonstrates the extent to which it is easier to pass a law than to abrogate it. But wouldn't it precisely be the role of a minister of justice to address the possibility of abrogating a law that goes against some of the most fundamental principles of democracy? Regardless of her motives to not openly side against the current state of denaturalization law, it is worth stressing the recurrent tenacity of denaturalization. A parallel with the political position taken by the provisional government at the wake of World War II comes to the fore. At that time, and as discussed in chapter 7, the provisional government annulled all denaturalization decrees proclaimed during World War II based on moral grounds because they saw in practices of denaturalization the result of totalitarian politics. But they neglected to abrogate the law on denaturalization altogether, coming back to its provisions as stated in the law of before the war. Accordingly, they perpetuated denaturalization's differentiating principle according to which native-borne nationals enjoy an irrevocable right to nationality, whereas new nationals only have access to conditional national identity and citizenship rights. Similarly, those who opposed Hollande's proposition to extend the field of denaturalization practices stressed the importance of the principle of equality before the law, affirming values of equality and diversity. Nonetheless, the debate was strikingly silent about the existing juridical configuration making denaturalization practices possible *already*. Prominent journalistic sources, such as the daily paper *Le Monde*, occasionally mentioned the fact that Hollande's reform was not inventing denaturalization's principle of differentiation but merely increasing it (Vaudano 2016). Whispers during a thunderstorm, these sporadic observations about the existing law were submerged by the noise of the debate about future plans. Somehow, the collective debate seems not ready to see and admit the fundamental weakness of France's republican ideal in its current state.

FROM PUBLIC DEBATE BACK TO SILENCE: SPECTERS OF DENATURALIZATION

On March 30, 2016, Hollande officially announced the aborting of his constitutional reform plan due to an unbridgeable disagreement between the two chambers of Parliament. The major point of disagreement revolved around the differentiating principle of denaturalization: since the European Convention on Human Rights and EU law prohibit any act of state to render a citizen stateless, France could only extend the provisions on practices of denaturalization by making the distinction between mono- and bi-nationals central. The government and the *Assemblée nationale* had tried to silence the distinction by rhetorically simply leaving it out of the bill text. But the *Sénat* worked through the rhetorical maneuver and restated the principle of equality as central, thereby making it fundamentally impossible for the *Assemblée* to take the reform further ("Inscrire l'État d'Urgence et La Déchéance de Nationalité Dans La Constitution" 2016). Like a storm passing, the debate on denaturalization was closed with Hollande's renunciation of his constitutional reform. Silence ensued, bringing denaturalization practices back to their characteristic latency.

It is this silence that has gained territory in President Macron's politics of security, centered so far on a new counterterrorism law (France 2017b). Promulgated on October 30, 2017, this new law concentrates on two main objectives: 1) to enable the state to end the state of emergency and 2) to endow the state with new means of common law "making it possible to better prevent terrorist threats outside of the state of emergency" (France 2017a). Most salient about this law is the fact that it has succeeded in incorporating elements of the provisional state of emergency into common law (Perret and Burgess 2017). The law thereby recalls Agamben's thesis on states of exception (1997), whose main theoretical point states that "the state of exception thus ceases to be referred to an external and provisional state of factual danger and comes to be confused with juridical rule itself" (108). Although such counterterrorism measures remain a topic for research and debate, this book's focus on denaturalization calls for another set of questions. It is in fact striking that this new counterterrorism law does not engage denaturalization practices; denaturalization is simply ignored. But is denaturalization thereby no longer relevant?

From a genealogical perspective, I find such absence meaningful for several reasons. Despite the context being utterly different, it first of all recalls the dynamics observed at the brink of World War II when, although denaturalization practices where being legitimized based on arguments about security, it did not appear in the list of measures to be taken against people deemed a threat to national security (chapter 6). This only confirms the fact that denaturalization is symbol politics indeed. Despite its initial appearance, that is, its systematic entwinement with arguments making use of security as a referential framework, denaturalization is not a tool that seems to have security in mind; it is rather a technology of government that achieves other ends. A speech act performing through the law on national citizenship, denaturalization represents a particular way of talking about socio-political concerns. It is a system of thought that influences seminal cultural political values, such as community, nationality, citizenship, selfhood, and otherness.

Furthermore, knowing the genealogy of denaturalization practices, denaturalization's relative silence in the most recent counterterrorism measure in France further points at the dynamics of political processes according to which dynamics of visibility and invisibility are constitutive of how political norms perform throughout history. When a norm proves to persist *and* to disseminate throughout times of crisis, as denaturalization does, its momentary invisibility is no longer an indication of a likely future disappearance, but rather of a haunting presence that continues to affect those political juridical norms attached to it. Not only has denaturalization proven to be persistent in dynamics of belonging and repression in the French nation-state throughout history, its narrative has become an international phenomenon. In effect, denaturalization law hasn't been abolished, but instead kept in the shape that we already know of. Furthermore, denaturalization is spreading internationally: As Matthew Gibney (2017, 366) reports,

> In the US, a number of politicians have proposed legislation calling for terrorists to be stripped of their citizenship on ground of joining foreign terrorist organizations ostensibly at war with the US. ... [New] legislation has emerged in Canada, Austria, the Netherlands and Belgium (and is proposed in many other countries) to deal with Islamist extremist terrorist organizations, particularly after the beginning of the war in Syria in 2011.

Clearly, denaturalization is far from disappearing. At most, it has gone under water, yet continuing to provoke those affective rippling effects spreading upon the ways in which norms of nationality and citizenship perform.

Seeing denaturalization's current state as a phenomenon of haunting history provides avenues to think about its position in contemporary and international politics of security. Present yet hardly perceptible, denaturalization behaves as a ghost (re)visiting the institutions of nationality and citizenship. As Esther Peeren and María del Pilar Blanco (2013) have noted, the figure of the ghost yields a fruitful conceptual metaphor that allows talking about traumatic memories of our cultural, political, and affective past in its relation to our present and future. The ghost yields traces of trauma; it operates in the uncanny space of ambiguous emotions, opacity being its first ally. Referring to Derrida's conceptualization of the specter (Derrida 1994), Peeren and Blanco further qualify the ghost as "operating on a number of temporal planes, most crucially the future and its possible interaction with the present and the past" (16). As a *revenant*, the ghost invokes what was; as an *arrivant*, it announces what will come; its particularity precisely lies in always being both at the same time (16): it brings sensations of the past into the present while coloring the ways in which we apprehend the future. In that sense, the haunting presence of the ghost yields a historical consciousness that forces us to "refigure the relation of the present to the past, how we might articulate the mass and force of the past in the present when they can no longer be captured by a progressive narrative" (Brown 2001, 139). In other words, the ghost's historical consciousness comes and disturbs dominant narratives of linear history: by making us look "into those matters that are considered not to matter" (Peeren and Blanco 2013, 11), a ghostly presence "questions the formation of knowledge itself and specifically invokes what is placed outside of it, excluded from perception and, consequently, from both the archive as the depository of the sanctioned, acknowledged past and politics as the (re)imagined present and future" (11).

Since denaturalization is not dead but merely latent, its position in national and international politics calls for awareness of its haunting presence within the formation of knowledge about nationality and citizenship. At the threshold between past, present, and future, denaturalization has the characteristic of escaping fields of visibility while at the same time remaining an active technology of government that shapes norms of belonging and repression. Its genealogy gives us cues to the ways in which it activates future political imaginations in its interaction with the present and the past. As an *arrivant*, announcing what will come, denaturalization represents a test for politics of nationality and citizenship. In the context of national and global insecurity, the political will to denaturalize those deemed a fundamental threat to national and/or global security openly challenges fundamental republican and democratic principles. Ensnared in rhetorical arguments centered on emergency and legitimized in the name of exception(s), denaturalization law provides administrative governmental powers with questionable room for maneuvering when it comes to deciding who is a citizen and who is not or ceases to be one. As a *revenant*, invoking what was, denaturalization reveals a technology of government that has accomplished the "conquest of the state by the nation" (Arendt 1973, 230). As one of the consequential residues of affective technologies governing institutional and geographical boundaries through nationality law, denaturalization yields historical traces of the ways in which the state has instituted modes of repression through the particularity of nationality rights. Its genealogy indicates that through denaturalization's affective constitution, the definition of terror, the terrorist, and terrorism asphyxiate the category of the stranger. While the deprivation of rights appears as an answer to collective fears, denaturalization turns into foreigners those prosecuted in the name of national security.

Haunting as it is, such historical consciousness remains characteristically excluded from mainstream political perception. As once more demonstrated by François Hollande's political memoirs (Hollande 2018), published just in time to enter the intertextual field of my arguments, the specters of denaturalization have yet to be exposed. Coming back to his years in power, Hollande confesses that his first regret is not having listened to Christiane Taubira on the question of denaturalization. He regrets "having underestimated the emotional impact of denaturalization." Politics is not always rational, he admits, and he should have known better and listened more attentively to the passionate pleas of opponents to his constitutional reform. Nonetheless, he stresses that he remains convinced that, from a rational point of view, the measure he proposed was a just one and in line with the republican value of equality, since denaturalization "can only target 'terrorists.'" Hollande has not only underestimated the emotional impact of denaturalization on the population during the debates following his propositions of constitutional reform, but he continues to underestimate the affective economy that has informed the logic of denaturalization from the start; he remains oblivious to the affective economy at work in the definition of "terrorism," and to the affective genealogy of those juridical political norms according to which the words defining the boundaries between the good citizens and those constituting a fundamental threat to the nation shift. What the genealogy of denaturalization shows is precisely that its political juridical normative criteria yields the historical consciousness of the extent to which affective norms participate in the definition of who is a citizen and who is not or ceases to be. Becoming aware of such history remains a political struggle, and a task for our politics to come.

NOTES

1. Such security rhetoric is in continuation with Sarkozy's controversial attitude following the riots affecting the Paris suburbs in 2005. Then interior minister, Sarkozy had pledged a zero-tolerance policy toward urban violence. He was, among others, criticized for referring to the rioters as "*racaille*" [rabble].

2. Sarah Perret's work on naturalization legislation in France, Germany, and the United States (2015) provides complementary insights to understanding the processes through which national citizenship is caught up in securitization processes.

3. In the event the person in question has been convicted "for an act which qualifies as a crime or an offense that undermines the fundamental interests of the nation, or for a crime or an offense constituting an act of terrorism," the time limit for a denaturalization decree to be issued is currently fifteen years, beginning at the date the individual was naturalized (French civil code, article 25-1) (France 1998).

4. The bill presented by M. Meunier was debated in the parliament on December 4, 2014, and rejected. The two remaining bills have not been discussed in the parliamentary assembly yet (as of March 2018), neither under Hollande's government nor under Macron's.

Conclusion

By paying attention to denaturalization in French politics of national citizenship, this book aims to attach the history of denaturalization to the political task of "knowing our ill body and bodies" (Brown 2001, 109); it introduces the possibility of a different understanding of those political juridical categories of nationality and citizenship through which we define ourselves. Taking denaturalization's genealogy into account destabilizes norms of citizenship and nationality as a purely rational and administrative exercise of state authority. Instead, this genealogy reveals that institutional norms of citizenship and nationality are the performative outcome of denaturalization as an affective technology of government.

Overall, denaturalization generates a specific mode of identifying those perceived as "other." Most visibly framed through security in response to times of crisis (chapter 9), its history also brings to light a more subtle governmental form of address. Throughout the chapters, we have seen the extent to which denaturalization goes hand in hand with an affective mechanism of rejection and repression that primarily works through a "metonymic slide" (Ahmed 2004a, 2004b). Based on relationships of associations, metonymic slides provoke signs to move between objects and bodies, applying the term of one thing to another "because of a recurrent relationship in common experience" (Abrams 1999, 99). As Ahmed puts it (2004a, 127), metonymic slides shape the surface of the collective body while "[attributing] others with emotional value, ... as being fearsome." For instance, the case of Mr. Scholler, a man of foreign origin who was arrested on French territory in 1793 and deported on the basis of his foreignness (chapter 2), showed the extent to which his status as foreigner became associated with a perception of threat to the Republic despite the lack of evidence against him. In a time when the political juridical order of France was being radically reshaped, the socio-political body was impregnated with feelings of fear and suspicion against those who might put the revolutionary project at risk. In such context, the term "foreigner" underwent two main transformations. It first of all shifted from a multi-sided definition designating a wide range of behaviors, professions, or affiliations to a narrow understanding of the foreigner as coming from outside the French metropolitan territory. Simultaneously, the term "foreigner" became aligned against the collective body and associated with that which was threatening. In that context, administrative practices and special police forces charged with the task of controlling people of foreign origin became sites where the "conquest of the state by the nation" (Arendt 1973, 230) was revealed, with important consequences for citizenship as a juridical political category. Ensnared in the performative force of juridical political practices within which language and emotions cohabit as they shape the surface of the national community, citizenship indeed was narrowed down from a potentially universal idea toward a nationalized mode of belonging.

These dynamics of belonging and repression express the extent to which "affect is constitutive of, and channeled into, practices of governance" (Fortier 2016, 1042). Although kept in the margins for long, the consideration of affect and emotions in social political dynamics, dynamics of citizenship in particular, represents by now a growing mode of investigating power relations beyond their rational expressions (Di Gregorio and Merolli 2016; Fortier 2016). Within such an affective realm, denaturalization generates a specific discourse through which perceptions of security and insecurity are linked to questions of citizenship rights as framed by nation-states. A technology governing affective citizenship, denaturalization yields those political struggles that have drawn, contested, and revised the notion of citizenship along the ways in which the state came to operate as "an instrument of the nation" (Arendt 1973, 231).

What stands out is the extent to which denaturalization is used as a means to clean or even purify the nation of those being perceived as a threat. Hence, presenting itself as a form of authoritarian affect, denaturalization expresses our "totalitarian infection" (Arendt 1973): it endows the state with the possibility to revise the law's effective boundaries on an *ad hoc* basis, depending on the contingent perception of that which is threatening. Studying archival documents made it visible that denaturalization's mechanisms of contesting the boundaries of national citizenship, enacted from above, are systematically tied to moral and affective concepts. Embedded into law, the affective economies involved increase the law's flexibility and adaptability. Love, faithfulness, sincerity, and worthiness stand for the inclusive norm; terrorism, treason, and threats allude to that which must be ruled out of the national community. These are perhaps common sense criteria of inclusion and repression. But what seems to be common sense is far from self-explanatory. Our first intuition gets lost in the opacity of concepts with vague semantic content. For what does it mean to love in political and juridical terms? And what does it mean to be sincere? Inversely, what do we understand as treason? And for whom can someone be threatening?

Having such opaque and affective criteria authorizing denaturalization bears important consequences. Governing through affect appears to be a means to impose difference, rather than, as Monica Mookherjee suggested (2005, 36), a means to enhance differences while transforming and critiquing institutional forms of address. The language of denaturalization addresses new nationals differently from French-born nationals; it also addresses consenting citizens differently from dissenting ones. Denaturalization is not, and has never been, about gaining the trust and loyalties of citizens. Instead, as Hollande has (inadvertently) admitted when confessing his regret (chapter 9), denaturalization is about purifying the nation, as a political body; it is about expelling its enemies.

Hence, mobilizing nationality and citizenship rights in the name of national security, denaturalization presents the deprivation of rights as an answer to collective fear. Its history, which I have here traced back to the French Revolution, shows a number of fluctuations, which are powerful reminders of the contingency involved when some values of sovereignty become institutionalized, while simultaneously others are suppressed. The targeted subjects have changed labels over time: from Mr. Scholler to de Gaulle, from de Gouges to Olzanski, from Mr. Furcy to the unknown Jewish denaturalized citizens, from the collaborators to the "terrorist," we have seen that denaturalization operates politically and affectively, aligning its targeted subjects against the community while, at the same time, shaping the contours of that same community. A shifting normative border, denaturalization operates as the vector of political emotions traveling from governmental powers to political subjects—to us.

If, as Brown puts it (2001, 106), "the measure of genealogy's success is … [to tell] a story that disturbs our habits of self-recognition, posing an 'us' that is foreign," then I wish this genealogy to be successful. Knowing that France abolished the death penalty in 1981, civic degradation in 1994, and the category of "degrading punishment" [*peine infamante*] in 2003 (Simonin 2008, 681), historical consciousness about denaturalization's history may, in time, lead to abolishing denaturalization, too. Despite topical political developments currently going in the opposite direction, I remain inspired by Brown's perspective when she writes: "the point of genealogy is to map

the discourses and political rationalities constitutive of our time … such that
'that-which-is' can be thought as 'that-which-might-not-be.' Its point is to
introduce the possibility of a different discursive understanding of ourselves
and our possibilities" (112). Now, as we witness the rise of denaturalization in
global counterterrorism practices, I invite you, reader, to ask: "Who are we?"
and most importantly, "Who do we want to become?"

Bibliography

Abrams, M. H. 1999. *A Glossary of Literary Terms*. Seventh edition. Fort Worth: Harcourt Brace College Publishers.

Agamben, Giorgio. 1997. "The Camp as Nomos of the Modern." In *Violence, Identity, and Self-Determination*, edited by Hent de Vries and Samuel Weber, translated by Daniel Heller-Roazen, 106–18. Stanford: Stanford University Press.

———. 1998. *Homo Sacer: Sovereign Power and Bare Life*. Translated by Daniel Heller-Roazen. Stanford: Stanford University Press.

Ahmed, Sara. 2004a. "Affective Economies." *Social Text* 79 (2.2): 117–39.

———. 2004b. *The Cultural Politics of Emotion*. New York: Routledge.

Aïssaoui, Mohammed. 2011. *L'affaire de l'Esclave Furcy: Récit*. Paris: Gallimard.

Alix, Julie. 2010. *Terrorisme et Droit Pénal: Étude Critique Des Incriminations Terroristes*. Nouvelle Bibliothèque de Thèses. Paris: Dalloz.

American Embassy Paris. 2005. "French Judge Says C/T Focus Is on 'Jihadists to Iraq.' Cable Reference Id: #05PARIS3118." https://wikileaks.org/plusd/cables/05PARIS3118_a.html.

Amic, August, and Etienne Mouttet, eds. 1812. *Orateurs Politiques. Tribune Française. Choix Des Discours et Des Rapports Les plus Remarquables Prononcés Dans Nos Assemblées Parlementaires*. Volume 2. Paris: Mairet & Fourniers.

Anderson, Benedict. 2006. *Imagined Communities: Reflections on the Origin and Spread of Nationalism*. Revised edition. London: Verso.

Aradau, Claudia, and Jef Huysmans. 2014. "Critical Methods in International Relations: The Politics of Techniques, Devices and Acts." *European Journal of International Relations* 20 (3): 596–619. doi:10.1177/1354066112474479.

Arendt, Hannah. 1973. *The Origins of Totalitarianism*. New York: Harcourt Brace Jovanovich.

———. 1990. *On Revolution*. Reprinted. London: Penguin Books.

———. 2006. *Eichmann in Jerusalem: A Report on the Banality of Evil*. New York: Penguin Books.

Arosemena, Gustavo. 2014. "Human Rights." In *Introduction to Law*, edited by Jaap Hage and Bram Akkermans, 261–86. Cham, Switzerland: Springer International Publishing. doi:10.1007/978-3-319-06910-4_12.

Austin, John L. 1962. *How to Do Things with Words: The William James Lectures Delivered at Harvard University in 1955*. Edited by James O. Urmson. Cambridge, MA: Harvard University Press.

"Avalon Project—Declaration of the Rights of Man—1789." n.d. Accessed March 14, 2018. http://avalon.law.yale.edu/18th_century/rightsof.asp.

Balibar, Étienne. 1988. "Propositions on Citizenship." *Ethics* 98 (4): 723–30. doi: 10.1086/293001.

———. 1991. "Citizen Subject." In *Who Comes After the Subject?*, edited by Eduardo Cadava, Peter Connor, and Jean-Luc Nancy, 33–57. New York: Routledge.

———. 1998. *Droit de Cité*. Paris: Presses Universitaires de France.

Balibar, Étienne, and James Swenson. 2004. *We, the People of Europe? Reflections on Transnational Citizenship*. Princeton, NJ: Princeton University Press.

Balibar, Étienne, and Immanuel Maurice Wallerstein. 1991. *Race, Nation, Class: Ambiguous Identities*. London: Verso.

Bauböck, Rainer. 1994. *Transnational Citizenship: Membership and Rights in International Migration*. Aldershot, Hants, England: E. Elgar.

Bédarida, François. 1994. "De Gaulle and the Resistance 1940–1944." In *De Gaulle and Twentieth Century France*, edited by Hugh Gough and John Horne, 19–34. London: Edward Arnold.

Beiner, Ronald. 2000. "Arendt and Nationalism." In *The Cambridge Companion to Hannah Arendt*, edited by Dana Villa, 44–62. Cambridge: Cambridge University Press. doi:10.1017/CCOL0521641985.003.

Benhabib, Seyla. 2004. *The Rights of Others: Aliens, Residents and Citizens*. New York: Cambridge University Press.

Benhabib, Seyla, and Robert Post. 2006. *Another Cosmopolitanism*. Oxford: Oxford University Press.

Bhabha, Homi K., ed. 1990. *Nation and Narration*. New York: Routledge.

Bigo, Didier. 1991. "Les attentats de 1986 en France : Un Cas de Violence Transnationale et ses Implications (Partie 1)." *Cultures & conflits* (online) 04. doi:10.4000/conflits.129.

———. 2002. "Security and Immigration: Toward a Critique of the Governmentality of Unease." *Alternatives: Global, Local, Political* 27 (1 suppl): 63–92. doi:10.1177/03043754020270S105.

———. 2012. "Freedom and Speed in Enlarged Borderzones." In *The Contested Politics of Mobility: Borderzones and Irregularity*, edited by Vicki Squire, 31–50. London: Routledge.

Blanc, Olivier. 1993. "Introduction." In *Olympe de Gouges. Écrits Politiques 1792–1793*, edited by Olivier Blanc, 7–42. Paris: Côté-femmes.

Broekhoven, Lia van. 2013. "Speech by Lia van Broekhoven at CTITF Conference June 2013." Presented at the International Counter-Terrorism Focal Points Conference on Addressing Conditions Conducive to the Spread of Terrorism and Promoting Regional Cooperation, Geneva, Counter-Terrorism Implementation Task Force

Office, June 14. http://www.humansecuritynetwork.net/docview/-/asset_publisher/ faM5/content/speech-by-lia-van-broekhoven-at-ctitf-conference-june-2013/.

Brown, Wendy. 2001. *Politics out of History*. Princeton: Princeton University Press.

Brubaker, Rogers. 1992. *Citizenship and Nationhood in France and Germany*. Cambridge, MA: Harvard University Press.

Butler, Judith. 1993. *Bodies That Matter: On the Discursive Limits of "Sex."* New York: Routledge.

———. 1997. *Excitable Speech: A Politics of the Performative*. New York: Routledge.

———. 2009. *Frames of War: When Is Life Grievable?* London; New York: Verso.

Buzan, Barry, Ole Wæver, and Jaap de Wilde. 1998. *Security: A New Framework for Analysis*. Boulder, CO: Lynne Rienner.

Cadava, Eduardo, Peter Connor, and Jean-Luc Nancy, eds. 1991. *Who Comes after the Subject?* New York: Routledge.

Calafat, Guillaume. 2011. "Droit Pénal et États d'Exception. Entretien avec Anne Simonin." *Tracés*, no. 20 (May): 177–97. doi:10.4000/traces.5086.

Certeau, Michel de. 1984. *The Practice of Everyday Life*. Berkeley: University of California Press.

Césaire, Aimé. 1972. *Discourse on Colonialism*. Translated by Joan Pinkham. New York: Monthly Review Press.

———. 2004. *Victor Schoelcher et l'Abolition de l'Esclavage: Suivi de Trois Discours*. Lectoure: Editions le Capucin.

Chamoiseau, Patrick. 2002. *Écrire en Pays Dominé*. Paris: Gallimard.

Corbett, Edward P. J., and Robert J. Connors. 1999. *Classical Rhetoric for the Modern Student*. Fourth edition. New York: Oxford University Press.

Cour d'Appel de Paris. 2005. "Arrêt Du 14 Décembre 2005." www.cap-office.net/_ zfiles0/sos-attentats/EC9213197EAC4B54B1066F880BE7E983.pdf.

Cour Royale de Paris. 1844. "Plaidoyer de Mr E. Thureau Pour Le Sieur Furcy Indien." Bibliothèque nationale de France, Paris.

Critchley, Simon. 2011. "Is Utopianism Dead?" *Log* 22: 169–75.

Culler, Jonathan D. 2011. *Literary Theory: A Very Short Introduction*. Second edition, fully updated new edition. New York: Oxford University Press.

Derrida, Jacques. 1990. "Force of Law. The Mystical Foundation of Authority." Translated by Mary Quaintance. *Cardozo Law Review* 11 (9): 920–1045.

———. 1994. *Specters of Marx: The State of the Debt, the Work of Mourning, and the New International*. Translated by Peggy Kamuf. New York: Routledge.

Derrida, Jacques, and Anne Dufourmantelle. 2000. *Of Hospitality*. Translated by Rachel Bowlby. Stanford: Stanford University Press.

Di Gregorio, Michael, and Jessica L. Merolli. 2016. "Introduction: Affective Citizenship and the Politics of Identity, Control, Resistance." *Citizenship Studies* 20 (8): 933–42. doi:10.1080/13621025.2016.1229193.

"Djamel Beghal; Terroriste Ou Prisonier d'opinion?" 2013. Accessed January 10. https://freedjamelbeghal.wordpress.com/.

Farrier, David. 2011. *Post-Colonial Asylum: Seeking Sanctuary before the Law*. Liverpool: Liverpool University Press.

Fortier, Anne-Marie. 2016. "Afterword: Acts of Affective Citizenship? Possibilities and Limitations." *Citizenship Studies* 20 (8): 1038–44. doi:10.1080/13621025.20 16.1229190.

Foucault, Michel. 1982. *The Archaeology of Knowledge.* Translated by A. M. Sheridan Smith. New York: Pantheon Books.

———. 1990. *The History of Sexuality.* Translated by Robert Hurley. Volume I. New York: Vintage Books.

———. 2007a. *Security, Territory, Population: Lectures at the Collège de France, 1977–1978.* Edited by Michel Senellart. Translated by Graham Burchell. 1. New York: Picador.

———. 2007b. "What Is Critique?" In *The Politics of Truth,* edited by Sylvère Lotringer and Lysa Hochroth, translated by Lysa Hochroth, 41–82. New York: Semiotext(e).

France. n.d.-a. "Note Pour Monsieur Le Secrétaire Général." MS. 19950165/10 C 2698. Archives nationales, Pierrefitte-sur-Seine.

———. n.d.-b. "Projet de Loi." MS. 19950165/10 C 2698. Archives nationales, Pierrefitte-sur-Seine.

———. 1793. "Affaire Scholler. Tribunal Revolutionnaire." MS. W//276 d. 75. Archives nationales, Paris.

———. 1804. "Code Civil. Livre II : Des Biens et des Différentes Modifications de la Propriété. Titre II : De la Propriété. Article 544." Legifrance.gouv.fr. https://www. legifrance.gouv.fr/affichCodeArticle.do?idArticle=LEGIARTI000006428859&cid Texte=LEGITEXT000006070721&dateTexte=20180416.

———. 1848. "Décret du 27 Avril 1848 Relatif à l'Abolition de l'Esclavage dans les Colonies et Possessions Françaises." *Moniteur Universel. Journal Officiel de la République Française.* Archives Assemblée nationale, Paris.

———. 1918. "Note du Directeur." MS. 19950165/10 C 2698. Archives nationales, Pierrefitte-sur-Seine.

———. 1921. "Lettre du Préfet Des Alpes-Maritimes." MS. 19950165/10 C 2698. Archives nationales, Pierrefitte-sur-Seine.

———. 1932. "Dossier Thomas Olzanski." MS. BB/11/6489 di 41506x14. Archives nationales, Pierrefitte-sur-Seine.

———. 1939. "Annexe Nº 6356. Projet de Loi Tendant à la Ratification du Décret du 9 Septembre 1939 Modifiant les Dispositions Relatives à la Déchéance de la Nationalité Française." *Journal Officiel.* MICR M-35137. Bibliothèque nationale de France, Paris.

———. 1940a. "Loi du 22 Juillet 1940 Relative à la Révision Des Naturalisations." *Journal Officiel.* MICR D-10046. Bibliothèque nationale de France, Paris.

———. 1940b. "Loi du 23 Juillet 1940 Relative à la Déchéance de la Nationalité à l'Égard des Français qui Ont Quitté la France." *Journal Officiel.* MICR D-10046. Bibliothèque nationale de France, Paris.

———. 1941a. "Loi du 28 Février 1941 Modifiant la Loi du 23 Juillet 1940 Relative à la Déchéance de la Nationalité à l'Égard Des Français qui Ont Quitté la France." *Journal Officiel.* 19900353/1. Archives nationales, Pierrefitte-sur-Seine.

———. 1941b. "Loi du 8 Mars 1941 Relative à la Déchéance de la Nationalité à l'Égard des Français qui se Rendent dans Une Zone Dissidente." *Journal Officiel.* 19900353/1. Archives nationales, Pierrefitte-sur-Seine.

———. 1941c. "Loi du 2 Juin 1941 Remplaçant la Loi du 3 Octobre 1940 Portant Statut des Juifs." *Journal Officiel.* 19900353/1. Archives nationales, Pierrefitte-sur-Seine.

———. 1941d. "Loi du 18 Juillet 1941 Relative aux Mesures à Prendre à l'Égard des Individus Dangereux pour la Défense Nationale et la Sécurité Publique." *Journal Officiel.* 19900353/1. Archives nationales, Pierrefitte-sur-Seine.

———. 1943. "Ordonnance du 18 Avril 1943 Portant Abrogation des Lois Relatives à la Déchéance de la Nationalité Française." *Journal Officiel.* AJ/16/7128. Archives nationales, Pierrefitte-sur-Seine.

———. 1944a. "Discussion du Projet d'Ordonnance Instituant l'Indignité Nationale." *Journal Officiel.* MICR M-35134. Bibliothèque nationale de France, Paris.

———. 1944b. "Ordonnance du 26 Août 1944 Instituant l'Indignité Nationale." *Journal Officiel.* MICR M-35133. Bibliothèque nationale de France, Paris.

———. 1945. Procès du Maréchal Pétain. Compte Rendu *in extenso* des Audiences. Imprimerie des Journaux Officiels. Haute Cour de Justice, Paris.

———. 1950. "Annexe N° 10738. Proposition de Loi Tendant à Modifier Certaines Dispositions du Code La Nationalité et à Renforcer Les Mesures Interdisant l'Ingérence des Réfugiés et Ressortissant Étrangers dans les Affaires Intérieures de la France." *Journal Officiel.* 20000145/4. Archives nationales, Pierrefitte-sur-Seine.

———. 1951a. "Dossier Proposition de la Loi Hugues." MS. 20000145/4 C 5646. Archives nationales, Pierrefitte-sur-Seine.

———. 1951b. "Note du Ministère de La Santé Publique." MS. 20000145/4 C 5646. Archives nationales, Pierrefitte-sur-Seine.

———. 1958. "Constitution de la République Française." Assemblee-nationale.fr. http://www.assemblee-nationale.fr/connaissance/constitution.asp.

———. 1986. "Loi N° 86-1020 du 9 Septembre 1986 Relative à la Lutte Contre le Terrorisme." https://www.legifrance.gouv.fr/affichTexte.do?cidTexte=JORFTEXT 000000693912&categorieLien=id.

———. 1996. "Assemblée nationale. Séance du 18 Avril 1996." *Journal Officiel de la République Française.* http://archives.assemblee-nationale.fr/10/cri/10-1995-1996-ordinaire1.asp.

———. 1998. "Code Civil. Chapitre IV. Section 3: De la Déchéance de la Nationalité Française. Article 25." Legifrance.gouv.fr. https://www.legifrance. gouv.fr/affichCode.do?idSectionTA=LEGISCTA000006150513&cidTexte=LEGI TEXT000006070721&dateTexte=20161018.

———. 2010. "Séance En Hémicycle du 30 Sept. 2010. Immigration, Intégration, et Nationalité." http://www.assemblee-nationale.fr/13/cri/2009-2010-extra2/20102023.asp.

———. 2013. "Proposition de Loi Visant à Déchoir de la Nationalité Française Tout Individu Portant les Armes Contre les Forces Armées Françaises et de Police. N° 996." Assemblee-nationale.fr. http://www.assemblee-nationale.fr/14/propositions/pion0996.asp.

———. 2014a. "Proposition de Loi Visant à Élargir la Déchéance de la Nationalité Française. N° 1948." Assemblee-nationale.fr. http://www.assemblee-nationale.fr/14/propositions/pion1948.asp.

———. 2014b. "Proposition de Loi Visant à Permettre la Déchéance de la Nationalité pour Tout Combattant Djihadiste Français. N° 2016." Assemblee-nationale.fr. http://www.assemblee-nationale.fr/14/propositions/pion2016.asp.

———. 2016. "Code Pénal. Livre IV. Titre II. Chapitre Ier. Des Actes de Terrorisme. Article 421-1." Legifrance.gouv.fr. https://www.legifrance.gouv.fr/affichCode.do;jsessionid=60E5AA1CD55B431B7D32E1B75F8D7511.tplgfr38s_1?idSectionTA=LEGISCTA000006149845&cidTexte=LEGITEXT000006070719&dateTexte=20180308.

———. 2017a. "Loi 2017-1510. Communiqué de Presse Du Conseil Des Ministres Du 22 Juin 2017." Legifrance.gouv.fr. https://www.legifrance.gouv.fr/affichLoiPubliee.do?idDocument=JORFDOLE000034990290&type=general&legislature=15.

———. 2017b. "Loi N° 2017-1510 Du 30 Octobre 2017 Renforçant la Sécurité Intérieure et la Lutte Contre le Terrorisme." Legifrance.gouv.fr. https://www.legifrance.gouv.fr/affichLoiPubliee.do?idDocument=JORFDOLE000034990290&type=general&legislature=15.

———. 2018. "L'étendue Du Droit d'Accès—CADA." Accessed April 16. http://www.cada.fr/l-etendue-du-droit-d-acces,20.html.

Gellner, Ernest. 2009. *Nations and Nationalism*. Second edition. Ithaca, NY: Cornell University Press.

Gaulle, Charles de. 1954. *Mémoires de Guerre*. Paris: Plon.

Gerbeau, Hubert. 1996. "Les Libertés de Bourbon: D'une Revolution à l'Autre." In *Révolution Française et Océan Indien: Prémices, Paroxysmes, Héritages et Déviances: Actes Du Colloque de Saint-Pierre de La Réunion*, edited by Claude Wanquet and Benoît Jullien, 347–60. La Réunion; Paris: Université de La Réunion; L'Harmattan.

———. 2013. *Les Esclaves Noirs: Pour Une Histoire du Silence*. Paris: Les Indes savantes.

Gibney, Matthew J. 2017. "Denationalization." In *The Oxford Handbook of Citizenship*, edited by Ayelet Shachar, Rainer Bauböck, Irene Bloemraad, and Maarten Peter Vink. First edition, 358–82. New York: Oxford University Press.

Girard, René. 1986. *The Scapegoat*. Translated by Yvonne Freccero. Baltimore: Johns Hopkins University Press.

Goede, Marieke de. 2008a. "Beyond Risk: Premediation and the Post-9/11 Security Imagination." *Security Dialogue* 39 (2–3): 155–76. doi:10.1177/0967010608088773.

———. 2008b. "The Politics of Preemption and the War on Terror in Europe." *European Journal of International Relations* 14 (1): 161–85. doi:10.1177/1354066107087764.

———. 2012. *Speculative Security: The Politics of Pursuing Terrorist Monies*. Minneapolis: University of Minnesota Press.

Goede, Marieke de, and Samuel Randalls. 2009. "Precaution, Preemption: Arts and Technologies of the Actionable Future." *Environment and Planning D: Society and Space* 27 (5): 859–78. doi:10.1068/d2608.

Goody, Jack. 1986. *The Logic of Writing and the Organization of Society.* New York: Cambridge University Press.

Gouges, Olympe de. 1993a. *Écrits Politiques.* Edited by Olivier Blanc. Paris: Côté-femmes.

———. 1993b. "Les Trois Urnes." In *Écrits Politiques 1792–1793*, edited by Olivier Blanc, 123–48. Paris: Côté-femmes.

———. 1993c. "Olympe de Gouges au Tribunal Révolutionnaire." In *Écrits Politiques 1792–1793*, edited by Olivier Blanc, 245–60. Paris: Côté-femmes.

———. 1993d. "Une Patriote Persécutée à La Convention Nationale." In *Écrits Politiques 1792–1793*, edited by Olivier Blanc, 249–53. Paris: Côté-femmes.

———. 2012. *Déclaration des Droits de la Femme et de la Citoyenne; Suivi de Préface pour les Dames ou Le Portrait des Femmes.* Paris: Editions Mille et Une Nuits.

Gough, Hugh, and John Horne, eds. 1994. *De Gaulle and Twentieth Century France.* London: Edward Arnold.

Grandmaison, Olivier Le Cour. 2005. "L'exception et la Règle: Sur le Droit Colonial Français." *Diogène* 212: 42–64. doi:10.3917/dio.212.0042.

Guild, Elspeth. 2009. *Security and Migration in the 21st Century.* Cambridge, MA: Polity.

Guillaume, Xavier, and Jef Huysmans. 2013. "Introduction Citizenship and Security." In *Citizenship and Security: The Constitution of Political Being*, edited by Xavier Guillaume and Jef Huysmans, 1–17. New York: Routledge.

Halberstam, Judith. 2011. *The Queer Art of Failure.* Durham, NC: Duke University Press.

Hayes, Ben. 2012. "Counter Terrorism, 'Policy Laundering' and the FATF: Legalising Surveillance, Regulating Civil Society. Human Security Collective." Transnational Institute/Statewatch. http://www.hscollective.org/wp-content/uploads/2013/09/fatf-report.pdf.

Héran, François. 2011. "Law and Migration." Maison Descartes, Amsterdam, November 4.

Hirsch Ballin, Ernst. 2011. "Burgerrechten." Inaugural Lecture, University of Amsterdam, September 9. http://www.oratiereeks.nl/upload/pdf/PDF-2406weboratie_Hirsch_Balin2.pdf.

Hollande, François. 2015. "Déclaration de M. François Hollande, Président de La République, Devant Le Parlement Réuni En Congrès à La Suite Des Attaques Terroristes Perpétrées à Paris et En Seine-Saint-Denis, Versailles Le 16 Novembre 2015." Parlement Réuni en Congrès, Versailles, November 16. http://discours.vie-publique.fr/notices/157002982.html.

———. 2018. *Les Leçons Du Pouvoir.* eBook. Stock.

Honig, Bonnie. 2002. "A Legacy of Xenophobia." *Boston Review* (online) 27 (6). http://bostonreview.net/archives/BR27.6/honig.html.

Honohan, Iseult. 2017. "Liberal and Republican Conceptions of Citizenship." In *The Oxford Handbook of Citizenship*, edited by Ayelet Shachar, Rainer Bauböck, Irene Bloemraad, and Maarten Peter Vink. First edition, 83–106. New York: Oxford University Press.

Huysmans, Jef. 2000. "The European Union and the Securitization of Migration." *Journal of Common Market Studies* 38 (5): 751–77. doi:10.1111/1468-5965.00263.

———. 2006. *The Politics of Insecurity: Fear, Migration, and Asylum in the EU.* New York: Routledge.

———. 2014. *Security Unbound: Enacting Democratic Limits.* New York: Routledge.

"Inscrire l'État d'Urgence et La Déchéance de Nationalité Dans La Constitution." 2016. March 22. https://www.senat.fr/espace_presse/actualites/201602/inscrire_letat_durgence_et_la_decheance_de_nationalite_dans_la_constitution.html.

Isin, Engin F. 2002. *Being Political: Genealogies of Citizenship.* Minneapolis: University of Minnesota Press.

———. 2012. *Citizens without Frontiers.* New York: Continuum International Publishing Group.

———. 2017. "Performative Citizenship." In *The Oxford Handbook of Citizenship*, edited by Ayelet Shachar, Rainer Bauböck, Irene Bloemraad, and Maarten Peter Vink. First edition, 500–523. New York: Oxford University Press.

Isin, Engin F., and Peter Nyers. 2014. "Introduction: Globalizing Citizenship Studies." In *Routledge Handbook of Global Citizenship Studies*, edited by Engin F. Isin and Peter Nyers. Abingdon: Routledge.

Jabri, Vivienne. 2006. "War, Security and the Liberal State." *Security Dialogue* 37 (1): 47–64. doi:10.1177/0967010606064136.

Jansen, Yolande, Robin Celikates, and Joost de Bloois, eds. 2015. *The Irregularization of Migration in Contemporary Europe: Detention, Deportation, Drowning.* New York: Rowman & Littlefield International.

Keener, Frederick M. 1983. *The Chain of Becoming: The Philosophical Tale, the Novel, and a Neglected Realism of the Enlightenment: Swift, Montesquieu, Voltaire, Johnson, and Austen.* New York: Columbia University Press.

Koopman, Colin. 2013. *Genealogy as Critique: Foucault and the Problems of Modernity.* Bloomington: Indiana University Press.

Lagarde, Paul. 2011. *La Nationalité Française.* Fourth edition. Paris: Dalloz.

Laguerre, Bernard. 1988. "Les Dénaturalisés de Vichy." *Vingtième Siècle. Revue d'histoire* 20: 3–15.

Lambert, Charles. 1928. "Préface." In *Manuel de l'Étranger En France. La Naturalisation Selon La Loi Du 10 Août 1927*, edited by Jacques Lidji and A. Le Moal, 7–13. Paris: Recueil Sirey.

Landau-Brijatoff, Alix. 2013. *Indignes d'Être Français: Dénaturalisés et Déchus Sous Vichy.* Paris: Buchet-Chastel.

Larousse, Éditions. 2018. "Définitions : perfide—Dictionnaire de français Larousse." Accessed January 8. http://www.larousse.fr/dictionnaires/francais/perfide/59499.

Leun, Joanne van der. 2010. "Crimmigratie: Rede in Verkorte Vorm Uitgesproken bij de Aanvaarding van het Ambt van Hoogleraar Criminologie aan de Universiteit Leiden op Vrijdag 11 December 2009." Universiteit Leiden.

Lidji, Jacques, and A. Le Moal, eds. 1928a. "Loi Du 10 Août 1927." In *Manuel de l'Étranger En France, La Naturalisation Selon La Loi Du 10 Août 1927, Droits et Devoirs de l'étranger Avant et Après La Naturalisation. Déchéance. Formules. Renseignements Pratiques. Textes et Projets de Loi.* Paris: Recueil Sirey.

———, eds. 1928b. *Manuel de l'Étranger En France, La Naturalisation Selon La Loi Du 10 Août 1927, Droits et Devoirs de l'étranger Avant et Après La Naturalisation. Déchéance. Formules. Renseignements Pratiques. Textes et Projets de Loi.* Paris: Recueil Sirey.

Limouzy, Jacques. 1986. "Rapport N° 202, Assemblée nationale, Annexe au Procès-Verbal de la Séance Du 18 Juin 1986, Fait au Nom de la Commission des Lois Constitutionnelles … Sur le Projet de Loi Relatif à la Lutte contre le Terrorisme." *Journal Officiel de la République Française.* Microfiche M 35137. Bibliothèque nationale de France, Paris.

Macklin, Audrey. 2014. "Citizenship Revocation, the Privilege to Have Rights and the Production of the Alien." *Queen's L.J.* 40 (1): 1–54.

Malnoury, Louis, ed. 1915. *Les Dénaturalisations d'Anciens Sujets d'Allemagne, Autriche—Hongrie et Turquie. Commentaires de La Loi Du 7 Avril 1915.* Paris: Georges Roustan.

Mantu, Sandra. 2015. *Contingent Citizenship: The Law and Practice of Citizenship Deprivation in International, European and National Perspectives.* Leiden: Brill Nijhoff.

Marrus, Michael Robert, and Robert O. Paxton. 1995. *Vichy France and the Jews.* Stanford: Stanford University Press.

Marsaud, Alain. 1995. "Rapport N° 2406, Assemblée Nationale, Enregistré à la Présidence de l'Assemblée Nationale le 29 Novembre 1995, Fait au Nom de la Commission des Lois Constitutionnelles … Sur le Projet de Loi … Tendant à Renforcer la Répression du Terrorisme." *Journal Officiel de la République Française.* A2-MF-Armoire 00010. Bibliothèque nationale de France, Paris.

———. 1996. "Rapport N° 2638, Assemblée Nationale, Enregistré à La Présidence de l'Assemblée Nationale Le 13 Mars 1996, Fait au Nom de La Commission Des Lois Constitutionnelles … Sur Le Projet de Loi … Tendant à Renforcer La Répression Du Terrorisme." *Journal Officiel de la République Française.* A2-MF-Armoire 00010. Bibliothèque nationale de France, Paris.

Marshall, Thomas H. 1950. *Citizenship and Social Class.* Edited by Tom Bottomore. London: Pluto Press.

Masson, Paul. 1996. "Rapport N° 178, Sénat, Session Ordinaire de 1995-1996, Annexe au Procès-Verbal de la Séance du 24 Janvier 1996, Fait au Nom de la Commission des Lois Constitutionnelles … Sur le Projet de Loi … Tendant à Renforcer la Répression du Terrorisme." *Journal Officiel de la République Française.* https://www.senat.fr/rap/l95-178/l95-1780.html.

Matthews, Dylan. 2013. "Everything You Need to Know about the Drone Debate." *Washington Post,* March 8.

Michel, Henri. 1980. *Histoire de La France Libre.* Fourth edition. Paris: Presses Universitaires de France.

Mookherjee, Monica. 2005. "Affective Citizenship: Feminism, Postcolonialism and the Politics of Recognition." *Critical Review of International Social and Political Philosophy* 8 (1): 31–50. doi: 10.1080/1369823042000335830.

Mornet, André. 1949. *Quatre Ans à Rayer de Notre Histoire.* Paris: Éditions Self.

Morrison, Toni. 1993. "Nobel Lecture." *Nobelprize.org*. December 7. https://www. nobelprize.org/nobel_prizes/literature/laureates/1993/morrison-lecture.html.

Nairn, Tom. 1997. *Faces of Nationalism: Janus Revisited*. London: Verso.

Noiriel, Gérard. 1998. *Réfugiés et Sans-Papiers: La République Face au Droit d'Asile; XIXe–XXe siècle*. Paris: Hachette.

———. 2005. *État, Nation et Immigration: Vers Une Histoire du Pouvoir*. Paris: Gallimard.

———. 2007. *À Quoi Sert l'Identité Nationale?* Marseille: Agone.

Nyers, Peter. 2003. "Abject Cosmopolitanism: The Politics of Protection in the Anti-Deportation Movement." *Third World Quarterly* 24 (6): 1069–93. doi:10.1080/01 436590310001630071.

———. 2008. "In Solitary, in Solidarity: Detainees, Hostages and Contesting the Anti-Policy of Detention." *European Journal of Cultural Studies* 11 (3): 333–49. doi:10.1177/1367549408091847.

———. 2011. "Forms of Irregular Citizenship." In *The Contested Politics of Mobility: Borderzones and Irregularity*, edited by Vicki Squire, 184–98. New York: Routledge.

Orwell, George. 1989. *Animal Farm*. London: Penguin Modern Classics.

Peabody, Sue. 2017. *Madeleine's Children: Family, Freedom, Secrets, and Lies in France's Indian Ocean Colonies*. eBook. New York: Oxford University Press.

Peeren, Esther, and María del Pilar Blanco. 2013. "Introduction: Conceptualizing Spectralities." In *The Spectralities Reader: Ghosts and Haunting in Contemporary Cultural Theory*, edited by María del Pilar Blanco and Esther Peeren, 1–34. eBook. New York: Bloomsbury Academic.

Peeren, Esther, and Anette Hoffmann. 2010. "Introduction: Representation Matters." *Thamyris/Intersecting* 20: 9–30.

Perret, Sarah. 2015. "Les Législations en Matière de Naturalisation: Vecteur de Sécuritisation des Politiques d'Immigration en Allemagne, aux États-Unis et en France." PhD dissertation, Université Paris-Saclay. https://tel.archives-ouvertes.fr/ tel-01278029/document.

Perret, Sarah, and J. Peter Burgess. 2017. "La Lutte Contre Le Terrorisme: Une Gouvernance Par l'Incertitude?" *TheConversation*. September 27. https:// theconversation.com/la-lutte-contre-le-terrorisme-une-gouvernance-par-lincertitude-84713.

Rancière, Jacques. 2004. "Who Is the Subject of the Rights of Man?" *The South Atlantic Quarterly* 103 (2/3): 297–310.

Rapport, Michael. 2000. *Nationality and Citizenship in Revolutionary France: The Treatment of Foreigners 1789–1799*. New York: Clarendon. http://www.myilibrary. com?id=44573.

Renan, Ernest. 1990. "What Is a Nation?" In *Nation and Narration*, edited by Homi K. Bhabha, 8–22. New York: Routledge.

Roman, Louis. 1941. *La Perte de la Nationalité Française à Titre de Déchéance. Thèse pour le Doctorat*. Marseille: Marcel Leconte.

Rosello, Mireille. 2001. *Postcolonial Hospitality: The Immigrant as Guest*. Stanford: Stanford University Press.

Sahlins, Peter. 2004. *Unnaturally French: Foreign Citizens in the Old Regime and After*. Ithaca, NY: Cornell University Press.

Sala-Molins, Louis. 1987. *Le Code Noir, ou, Le calvaire de Canaan*. Paris: Presses Universitaires de France.

Sarkozy, Nicolas. 2010. "Discours Sur Le Thème de La Lutte Contre l'Insécurité." July 30. http://www.dailymotion.com/video/xebbz2.

Scott, David. 1995. "Colonial Governmentality." *Social Text* 43: 191–220. doi:10.2307/466631.

"Secret of Justice." 2013. The Bureau of Investigative Journalism. https://v1.thebureauinvestigates.com/category/projects/secret-justice/.

Sedgwick, Eve Kosofsky. 1997. "Paranoid Reading and Reparative Reading." In *Novel Gazing: Queer Readings in Fiction*, edited by Eve Kosofsky Sedgwick, 1–37. Durham, NC: Duke University Press.

Siess, Jürgen. 2005. "Un Discours Politique Au Féminin. Le Projet d'Olympe de Gouges." *Mots. Les Langages Du Politique* 78: 9–21.

Simonin, Anne. 2008. *Le Déshonneur dans la République: Une Histoire de l'Indignité, 1791–1958*. Paris: B. Grasset.

Smolar, Piotr. 2010. "Wikileaks: Comment Washington Voit la Lutte contre le Terrorisme en France." *Le Monde*, November 29. http://www.lemonde.fr/international/article/2010/11/29/wikileaks-comment-washington-voit-la-lutte-contre-le-terrorisme-en-france_1446622_3210.html.

Stumpf, Juliet. 2006. "The Crimmigration Crisis: Immigrants, Crime, and Sovereign Power." *American University Law Review* 56 (2): 367–418.

———. Taubira, Christiane.2016a. "Je Quitte Le Gouvernement." Press Conference, Minister of Justice, Paris, January 27. http://www.lemonde.fr/politique/article/2016/01/27/la-ministre-de-la-justice-christiane-taubira-a-demissionne_4854309_823448.html.

———. 2016b. *Murmures à La Jeunesse*. Paris: Philippe Rey.

———. 2016c. "Parfois Résister c'est Rester, Parfois Résister c'est Partir. Par Fidélité à Soi, à Nous. Pour le Dernier Mot à l'Éthique et au Droit," January 27. https://twitter.com/ChTaubira/status/692259706572795905.

Thomas, Yan. 2011. *Les Opérations du Droit*. Edited by Marie-Angèle Hermitte and Paolo Napoli. Paris: Seuil/Gallimar.

Valluy, Jérôme. 2008. "Du Retournement de l'Asile (1948–2008) à la Xénophobie de Gouvernement : Construction d'un Objet d'Étude." *Cultures & Conflits* 69: 81–111.

Vanpée, Janie. 1999. "Performing Justice: The Trials of Olympe de Gouges." *Theatre Journal* 51 (1): 47–65.

Vaudano, Maxime. 2016. "Des Attentats de Novembre au Renoncement : Comment le Débat sur la Déchéance de Nationalité s'Est Enlisé." *Le Monde.fr*, January 6. http://www.lemonde.fr/les-decodeurs/article/2016/01/06/le-debat-sur-la-decheance-de-nationalite-explique-en-textos_4842673_4355770.html.

Wæver, Ole. 1995. "Securitization and Desecuritization." In *On Security*, edited by Ronnie D. Lipschutz, 46–86. New York: Columbia University Press.

Wahnich, Sophie. 2002. "De l'Économie Émotive de la Terreur." *Annales. Histoire, Sciences Sociales* 57 (4): 889–913.

———. 2010a. *L'Impossible Citoyen: L'Étranger dans le Discours de la Révolution Française*. Paris: Albin Michel.

———. 2010b. "Postface." In *L'Impossible Citoyen: L'Étranger dans le Discours de la Révolution Française*, i–xxii. Paris: Albin Michel.

Weil, Patrick. 2008. *How to Be French: Nationality in the Making since 1789*. Translated by Catherine Porter. Durham, NC: Duke University Press.

———. 2013. *The Sovereign Citizen: Denaturalization and the Origins of the American Republic*. First edition. Philadelphia: University of Pennsylvania Press.

Winter, Jay, and Antoine Prost. 2013. *René Cassin and Human Rights: From the Great War to the Universal Declaration*. Cambridge: Cambridge University Press.

Woods, Chris, Alice K. Ross, and Oliver Wright. 2013. "British Terror Suspects Quietly Stripped of Stripped of Citizenship … then Killed by Drones." *The Independent*, February 28.

Zalc, Claire. 2016. *Dénaturalisés. Les retraits de nationalité sous Vichy*. eBook. Paris: Éditions du Seuil. http://banq.pretnumerique.ca/accueil/isbn/9782021326437.

Index